Redis Essentials

Definitive Reference for Developers and Engineers

Richard Johnson

Contents

1 Redis Architecture and Design Principles   **5**

1.1   In-Memory Data Model   5

1.2   Core Command Processing   9

1.3   Persistence Mechanisms: RDB, AOF, and Hybrid .   12

1.4   Replication Internals   16

1.5   Sentinel and Automatic Failover Architecture   19

1.6   Cluster Mode and Partitioning   22

1.7   Event Notification and Pub/Sub System   25

2 Advanced Redis Data Structures   **29**

2.1   Strings, Bitmaps, and Bitfields   29

2.2   Lists and Streams   32

2.3   Hashes, Sets, and Sorted Sets   36

2.4   HyperLogLog and Probabilistic Structures   40

2.5   Geospatial Indexes   43

2.6   Stream Consumer Groups   47

3 Extending Redis: Scripting and Modules   **53**

    3.1   Lua Scripting Engine 53

    3.2   Transaction Semantics and Pipelining 56

    3.3   Redis Modules API 59

    3.4   Custom Data Structures in Modules 63

    3.5   Sandboxing and Security in Scripting 68

    3.6   Performance Considerations for Extensions 71

4 Scaling, High Availability, and Disaster Recovery   **77**

    4.1   Replicated and Partitioned Topologies 77

    4.2   Redis Cluster Administration 82

    4.3   Sentinel Best Practices 86

    4.4   Geo-Distributed Redis Deployments 89

    4.5   Disaster Recovery Planning 94

    4.6   Consistency and Fault Tolerance 99

5 Performance Engineering and Monitoring   **103**

    5.1   Memory Management and Eviction Policies 104

    5.2   Profiling and Benchmarking Redis Systems 107

    5.3   Latency Analysis and Optimization 110

    5.4   Hot Keys, Hot Slots, and Load Imbalance 114

    5.5   Operational Metrics and Instrumentation 118

    5.6   Advanced Logging and Tracing 122

6 Security, Access Control, and Compliance   **127**

6.1   Authentication and Role-Based Access Control . . . **127**

6.2   Encryption in Transit and at Rest **131**

6.3   Network Isolation and Firewalls **137**

6.4   Vulnerability Management and Hardening **140**

6.5   Auditing and Compliance Reporting **144**

7   **Redis in Modern Application Architectures**   **149**

7.1   Microservices and Service Discovery **149**

7.2   Caching Strategies **153**

7.3   Event-Driven and Real-Time Systems **156**

7.4   Session Management and User State **160**

7.5   Distributed Locking and Coordination **164**

7.6   Rate Limiting and Throttling **169**

8   **Integrations and Ecosystem**   **175**

8.1   Connecting   from   Diverse   Programming
Environments **175**

8.2   Integration with Cloud Services **180**

8.3   Observability and Monitoring Ecosystem **184**

8.4   Orchestrating Redis with Containers and Kubernetes **189**

8.5   Data Migration and ETL Pipelines **194**

8.6   Redis in the Serverless Ecosystem **197**

9   **Emerging Patterns and Future Directions**   **201**

9.1   Redis Beyond Cache: Primary Database Patterns . . **201**

5

9.2   AI/ML Feature Caching and Model Serving **204**

9.3   Edge and IoT Architectures **208**

9.4   Multi-Region and Multi-Cloud Redis **211**

9.5   Contributions from the Open Source Community . . **215**

9.6   The Roadmap: Redis in the Next Decade **218**

Introduction

Redis is a powerful, versatile, and high-performance in-memory data structure store that has become an indispensable tool in modern computing. This book, *Redis Essentials*, aims to provide a comprehensive and detailed exploration of Redis, covering its architecture, data structures, extensibility, operational considerations, and its role within contemporary application ecosystems.

This work is structured to offer both foundational insights and advanced technical knowledge. It begins by examining the core architectural principles that underpin Redis, including its in-memory data model, command processing mechanisms, and persistence strategies. Understanding these elements is critical for leveraging Redis effectively, as they directly influence performance characteristics such as latency, throughput, and fault tolerance. The book further delves into the intricacies of replication, failover, and cluster management, providing a thorough overview of Redis's design for availability and scalability.

In addition to architecture, this volume offers an in-depth treatment of Redis's advanced data structures. Readers will gain an understanding of fundamental types such as strings, lists, hashes, and sets, as well as specialized structures like streams, hyperloglogs, and geospatial indexes. The discussion includes their internal representations, performance considerations, and practical usage scenarios, enabling users to select appropriate data types and design effective workflows.

Recognizing Redis's capacity for extension, this book covers scripting and module development at length. It provides guidance on utilizing the Lua scripting engine for atomic and complex operations,
and explores the Redis Modules API for building custom functionalities in C. Attention is given to security, sandboxing, and performance aspects of these extensions, ensuring that readers can safely
and efficiently expand their Redis deployments to meet evolving
requirements.

Operational excellence is addressed through detailed examination
of scaling techniques, high availability configurations, and disaster
recovery planning. The book discusses best practices for cluster
administration, sentinel deployments, geo-distributed topologies,
and consistency models. These insights are crucial for designing resilient systems capable of maintaining integrity and performance
under diverse failure conditions.

Performance engineering and monitoring are essential for production environments, and this text devotes significant focus to memory management, latency optimization, workload balancing, and
observability. It outlines methodologies for profiling, benchmarking, and diagnosing performance challenges, supported by strategies for logging and tracing that facilitate root cause analysis.

Security considerations form another core theme, with comprehensive treatment of authentication, access control, encryption,
network isolation, vulnerability management, and compliance auditing. By integrating these practices, users can protect sensitive
data and maintain secure Redis operations in complex infrastructure landscapes.

The role of Redis within modern architectural paradigms is ex-
plored extensively. Topics include integration with microservices,
advanced caching strategies, event-driven systems, session management, and distributed coordination. The book also addresses

API rate limiting and throttling as essential mechanisms for service reliability and abuse prevention.

Lastly, this work surveys the rich ecosystem surrounding Redis, including client libraries across diverse programming languages, cloud service integrations, container orchestration, data migration, and serverless computing patterns. It concludes with a forward-looking perspective on emerging trends and future directions for Redis, highlighting innovations in database roles, AI/ML applications, edge computing, and multi-region deployments.

Redis Essentials is intended for developers, architects, and system engineers seeking a rigorous and practical understanding of Redis. Its comprehensive scope and technical depth equip readers to harness the full potential of Redis in building robust, scalable, and high-performance applications.

Chapter 1

Redis Architecture and Design Principles

Redis stands out in the world of data systems by following a unique set of architectural choices that prioritize performance, reliability, and simplicity. This chapter unveils the foundational principles that empower Redis to deliver blazing-fast speeds, seamless data durability, and robust high-availability—in ways that often defy conventional database wisdom. Dive into the internal mechanisms, from memory layouts to cluster partitioning, and discover how these design decisions shape every aspect of how Redis operates in production.

1.1. In-Memory Data Model

Redis's foundational architectural decision to maintain all data exclusively in main memory profoundly influences its performance profile and operational characteristics. By eschewing disk-based storage for the primary dataset, Redis achieves ultra-low latency in data access and manipulation, positioning itself as a leading technology for real-time applications. This section examines the implications of the in-memory data model, including its advantages in speed, the complexity of memory management, allocation strategies, memory efficiency considerations, and the attendant trade-offs.

At the core, storing data entirely in RAM enables Redis to bypass the inherently high latencies of traditional disk I/O operations. The memory access times-typically on the order of tens of nanoseconds-contrast sharply with the millisecond-level delays characteristic of even the fastest solid-state drives. Consequently, Redis supports sub-millisecond response times for both read and write operations, an essential feature for use cases such as caching layers, session stores, high-frequency messaging, leaderboards, and real-time analytics.

However, the adoption of an in-memory data model introduces significant resource constraints and design challenges. Main memory is more expensive and limited in capacity compared to disk storage, necessitating memory-efficient data structures, dynamic allocation schemes, and intelligent eviction policies to maintain performance and scalability. Redis addresses these challenges through a combination of compact encoding techniques and well-optimized allocation strategies tailored to its diverse data types.

Redis utilizes a variety of specialized data structures optimized for in-memory storage and manipulation. For instance, the String type is the most fundamental and often the most common; it stores sequences of bytes and can represent integers, floating-point numbers, or arbitrary binary data. Internally, Redis employs compact representations such as the Simple Dynamic String (SDS) structure, which includes metadata like the string length and allocation size to minimize the overhead during resizing operations. This structure facilitates efficient appends and avoids costly reallocations, balancing memory consumption with operational efficiency.

For more complex data types, Redis relies on tailored internal encodings chosen based on the size and nature of stored data. The List type, for example, can be encoded either as a linked list or a ziplist (a specially encoded contiguous array), depending on the total number of elements and their byte sizes. Ziplist encoding reduces memory footprint by storing elements contiguously, which improves cache locality and reduces pointer overhead, but at the cost of increased CPU cycles for insertions and deletions. Once the list exceeds certain thresholds (e.g., element count or total data size), Redis dynamically switches to a linked list to optimize performance for random insertions or removals. This adaptive encoding mechanism exemplifies the trade-off between memory efficiency and operational speed.

The Set type in Redis also adopts multiple encodings such as intset (integer set) and hashtable. The intset encoding is used for small sets containing only integer values; it represents the set as a sorted array of integers, utilizing minimal memory while supporting efficient membership checks with binary search. When the set grows or includes non-integer members, Redis transparently converts it to a hashtable-based representation, which sacrifices some memory efficiency for constant-time complexity on inserts, deletions, and membership checks. The dynamic transition between encodings reduces unnecessary memory consumption for small sets while maintaining speed and scalability.

Hash types in Redis have similar dual-encoding schemes. Small hashes are encoded using ziplists, where consecutive key-value pairs are tightly packed, reducing pointer overhead and minimizing fragmentation. When a hash grows or individual fields or values surpass given size thresholds, Redis migrates the encoding to a hashtable, enabling faster random access at the expense of higher memory usage. This approach reflects a fundamental principle in Redis's in-memory model: memory savings must not critically hamper average-case speed.

Memory allocation within Redis leverages efficient, scalable allocators designed to reduce fragmentation and speed up allocation and deallocation processes. Redis defaults to standard `malloc` implementations provided by the operating system; however, it can be configured to use `jemalloc` or other modern allocators optimized for multithreaded workloads and minimal fragmentation. Reducing fragmentation is pivotal in maintaining large, contiguous blocks of memory, which benefit both allocation performance and cache utilization during runtime.

The all-in-memory approach does impose inherent data size limitations dictated by the available system RAM. Consequently, Redis employs several strategies to handle datasets exceeding physical memory constraints. Key among these is its configurable eviction policies, which define how Redis decides to remove less recently or less frequently used data when approaching memory limits. Policies range from simple least-recently-used (LRU) to more sophisticated approximations like volatile LRU or time-to-live (TTL) based eviction, affording administrators fine-grained control within their specific operational contexts.

In addition, Redis supports various data persistence mechanisms, albeit asynchronously and without hindering in-memory operations. These mechanisms enable snapshotting and append-only file logging to durable storage, ensuring data durability in case of failure, while maintaining the performance benefits of an in-memory dataset. Still, the design explicitly separates persistence concerns from the in-memory model, reinforcing that the primary source of truth during runtime remains volatile RAM storage.

The speed-memory size trade-off is a defining characteristic for any in-memory datastore, and Redis exemplifies this balance through its architecture and implementation choices. For workloads demanding extreme low-latency access with manageable dataset sizes, Redis offers unparalleled performance. However, when datasets outgrow feasible memory limits or consistency constraints require complex durability models, other systems or hybrid approaches might be preferable.

Ultimately, Redis's in-memory data model encapsulates a set of deliberate design trade-offs. By prioritizing rapid access and update times through exclusively memory-resident data structures, combined with adaptive and efficient internal encodings, memory-aware allocation, and configurable eviction policies, Redis delivers a versatile platform positioned at the intersection of speed and memory constraints. These design elements enable its widespread adoption across domains that demand real-time responsiveness and flexible data handling within the physical bounds of available RAM.

1.2. Core Command Processing

The Redis server is architected around a single-threaded event loop that orchestrates the reception, parsing, execution, and response dispatch for client commands. This design choice underpins Redis's ability to deliver exceptionally high throughput with predictably low latency, despite its single-threaded nature. The core command processing pipeline hinges on three fundamental components: protocol serialization and parsing, request queuing and command dispatch, and concurrency management. Together, these elements create a tightly integrated processing model optimized for speed and simplicity.

At the forefront is the Redis Serialization Protocol (RESP), a lightweight and efficient wire protocol explicitly designed to minimize parsing complexity on the server side. Incoming client requests are transmitted as RESP arrays, where each element corresponds to a command token-either the command name or its arguments-encoded as bulk strings. The simplicity of RESP enables the Redis server to perform linear-time parsing by streaming input bytes directly into well-defined token boundaries. This parsing occurs incrementally within the event loop's read handler, handling partial data and preserving state until a complete command has been received.

Once a complete RESP command is parsed from a client's input buffer, it is enqueued into the server's command queue associated with that client connection. Despite Redis's single-threaded core, this queuing step is fundamental because it decouples input parsing from command execution, allowing the event loop to maintain responsiveness to network events while processing commands sequentially. The command queue typically resides in the client structure and holds fully parsed command objects, which include the command name, key arguments, and other parameters. This design facilitates later stages to process commands without re-parsing or reassembling token structures.

Command dispatch operates synchronously within the server's main event loop. When the event loop detects readiness for command execution, it dequeues the next command from the client's queue and invokes the associated command handler function. Command handlers are implemented as statically dispatched function pointers indexed by command names, enabling efficient command lookups via a hash table. This direct dispatch mechanism adds minimal overhead and supports rapid invocation of hundreds of distinct commands available in Redis.

Crucially, the entire command execution process-including key lookups, data modifications, and response serialization-occurs atomically within the event loop's single thread. This approach eliminates the need for complex concurrency control constructs such as locks or transactional isolation mechanisms. As a result, Redis guarantees strong consistency semantics for command execution, sidestepping race conditions common in multi-threaded databases. The single-threaded model permits direct and fast access to the in-memory dataset without synchronization overhead, thereby optimizing throughput.

To handle network I/O and temporal events without blocking, Redis relies on multiplexed event notification mechanisms provided by the operating system (such as epoll, kqueue, or select). The server's event loop continuously iterates, checking file descriptor readiness for read or write operations, and timer expirations for background tasks. During each iteration, the server performs the following sequence: it reads input data, parses commands, executes commands from client queues, and writes responses back to client sockets. This interleaved processing method prevents starvation of any client or task and enables high concurrency on a single CPU core.

Concurrency management in Redis transcends traditional multithreading paradigms through its cooperative multitasking within a single-threaded loop. Commands are executed back-to-back, and long-running operations are deliberately avoided or offloaded to asynchronous subsystems (such as persistence or cluster communication) to prevent event loop stalling. Additionally, Redis exposes non-blocking variants for commands that may otherwise impede responsiveness, maintaining a fluid command processing pipeline.

Redis also employs efficient request pipelining, where multiple commands are sent by clients without waiting for individual replies. The server buffers these requests, sequentially parses and enqueues them, then processes each command in turn, sending responses in order. This approach leverages the high-speed command processing pipeline to maximize network utilization while preserving command order semantics strictly.

Response serialization mirrors the efficiency of the input protocol. After command execution, the server serializes the reply into RESP format directly into the client output buffer. By reusing the RESP protocol and output buffering, Redis minimizes context switches and system calls involved in sending data back to clients, further reducing latency.

In summary, the Redis core command processing model is a carefully balanced system that capitalizes on a single-threaded, event-driven architecture aligned with a minimalistic binary protocol. This synergy between protocol simplicity, event-driven request handling, and non-blocking concurrency strategies enables Redis to achieve remarkably high command throughput while maintaining consistent and low response times.

1.3. Persistence Mechanisms: RDB, AOF, and Hybrid

Redis provides two principal mechanisms for persisting data to non-volatile storage: snapshotting, commonly implemented via RDB (Redis Database) files, and the append-only file (AOF) approach. Each method adopts fundamentally different strategies to balance the trade-offs among durability, performance, and recovery time, thus enabling Redis to serve diverse application requirements. This section elaborates on the operational principles, advantages, and limitations of both mechanisms, followed by an exploration of hybrid persistence configurations that harness their complementary strengths.

The RDB persistence strategy involves taking point-in-time snapshots of the entire dataset and serializing this to disk as a compact dump file. These snapshots occur either at specified intervals or when triggered explicitly by the user. Internally, Redis forks a child process which performs the serialization, leaving the parent process to continue servicing clients without blocking. This design ensures minimal interference with the in-memory workload.

Advantages:

- *Efficient Recovery:* RDB files provide a compact and fast-loading representation of the dataset, enabling quick data loading upon server restart.

- *Low Runtime Overhead:* Since snapshotting is infrequent

and occurs in a separate process, the runtime impact on the server's performance is modest.

- *Portability and Backup:* RDB files are self-contained and easily transferable between servers, facilitating backup and replication strategies.

Limitations:

- *Data Loss Window:* Because persistence occurs periodically, data created after the last snapshot but before a crash is lost, making RDB unsuitable for scenarios requiring fine-grained durability guarantees.

- *Snapshot Overhead on Large Datasets:* Although snapshotting is isolated, for very large datasets the fork operation incurs a high memory cost due to copy-on-write semantics, and the snapshotting frequency directly influences system memory usage patterns.

The AOF persistence mechanism logs every write operation received by Redis as a command appended to a dedicated file, thus creating a sequential record of state mutations. During recovery, Redis replays the command sequence to reconstruct the dataset exactly as it was.

AOF supports configurable fsync policies:

- `always` (synchronous): Every command write is flushed to disk immediately.

- `everysec` (default): The log is synced to disk once per second, balancing durability and performance.

- `no` (asynchronous): System dependent; delays fsync calls for best-effort durability.

Advantages:

- *Greater Durability:* With `always` or `everysec` sync, data loss windows are minimal or nearly eliminated.

- *Incremental Updates:* Unlike snapshotting, AOF rewrites occur asynchronously and incrementally, maintaining the log size without halting operations.

- *Human-Readable Format:* The append-only log contains Redis commands in textual format, aiding debugging and manual recovery when necessary.

Limitations:

- *Larger Storage Footprint:* The AOF file is generally larger than an equivalent RDB snapshot due to storing commands rather than a binary snapshot.

- *Slower Recovery Time:* Replaying the entire command log at startup is more time-consuming than loading an RDB snapshot, especially as the dataset and operation history grow.

- *Potential I/O Overhead:* Aggressive fsync policies induce increased disk I/O, potentially limiting throughput under high write loads.

Redis provides mechanisms to blend the advantages of RDB and AOF persistence, allowing configurations that optimize for both performance and durability. A primary hybrid strategy involves periodically creating RDB snapshots to compact the AOF log via an *AOF rewrite* process, which generates a minimal representation of the current dataset as an RDB snapshot embedded within the AOF. This reduces the file size and speeds up recovery while preserving the incremental durability benefits of AOF.

Recently, Redis introduced *hybrid persistence*, where the modified RDB format is extended to include recent command logs. This approach combines the snapshot's rapid load time with the AOF's granular durability, providing:

- *Faster Startup:* The hybrid persistence file contains a base snapshot followed by a small, appended log of recent changes, significantly reducing recovery time versus a full AOF replay.

- *Configurability:* Users can tune durability by adjusting snapshot frequency and the length of the appended log segment.

- *Lower Memory & I/O Pressure:* Forking and disk synchronization overheads are optimized via this incremental persistence model.

The selection of persistence mode and tuning of associated parameters must be driven by the application's tolerance for data loss, performance requirements, and operational environment:

- Applications requiring high throughput with relaxed durability constraints may prioritize RDB snapshots with infrequent intervals, leveraging the low overhead and fast recovery.

- Use cases demanding near-zero data loss should enable AOF persistence with `everysec` or `always` fsync, accepting higher I/O costs for durability.

- Hybrid persistence suits workloads needing low-latency startup combined with good durability guarantees, making it increasingly the default choice in modern Redis deployments.

Additionally, Redis allows simultaneous configuration of both RDB and AOF persistence, offering a fallback mechanism wherein the server restores first from AOF, falling back to RDB if no AOF is available. This dual-mode supports robust recovery strategies and flexible failover configurations in distributed architectures.

Redis's persistence mechanisms deliver a continuum of options enabling practitioners to finely tune the durability-performance trade-off. By understanding the fundamental attributes of snapshotting, append-only logging, and their hybridization, system architects can tailor Redis deployment characteristics optimally, matching the persistent state management to the demands of diverse real-time workloads.

1.4. Replication Internals

Redis replication operates on a fundamental master–replica paradigm designed to enhance data availability, redundancy, and read scalability in distributed environments. At the core of this mechanism is the unidirectional synchronization flow from a single master node to one or more replicas. Understanding the detailed processes of connection establishment, data transfer, and incremental synchronization is pivotal for architects designing fault-tolerant and high-throughput Redis deployments.

When a replica establishes a connection to a master, the protocol initiates a full state synchronization process unless an existing replication offset is compatible for partial resynchronization. The master maintains a replication backlog, a fixed-size circular buffer retaining a history of recent writes. This backlog allows replicas that temporarily lose connection to request only the missing data since their last known replication offset, thus avoiding the overhead of a full dataset transfer.

The initial handshake begins with the replica sending a PSYNC command complemented by the run ID and replication offset of its current dataset. Two outcomes are possible:

- **Full resynchronization (Full sync):** Occurs if the master cannot fulfill the partial resynchronization request, either due to a mismatch of the master's run ID or because the requested offset falls outside the backlog range. The master then creates a new replication ID and offset, forks a background child process to generate an RDB snapshot, and streams this snapshot to the replica. This snapshot encompasses the entire dataset, ensuring consistency. Upon synchronization completion, the master continues streaming incremental commands to maintain synchronization.

- **Partial resynchronization (PSYNC):** Executed if the master can satisfy the request. The master replies with a +CONTINUE status, followed immediately by the incremental command stream starting at the acknowledged offset. This process considerably reduces data transfer and synchronization time, particularly in large datasets or unstable network conditions.

The replication backlog size is a critical parameter influencing the feasibility of partial resynchronizations. A larger backlog allows replicas to rejoin the replication stream after prolonged disconnections without a full resync, enhancing system availability and reducing replication lag. However, it also requires more memory on the master node. Configurations must balance memory constraints and replication robustness.

Replication in Redis inherently supports asynchronous propagation of write commands, providing scalability for read operations by offloading reads to replicas without blocking the master. However, this introduces eventual consistency since replicas apply write commands with some delay. The replication link is nonblocking and entirely decoupled from client interactions on the master, thus preventing write operations from stalling due to replication delays.

Redis implements a replication offset mechanism to track the progress of data synchronization. Both master and replicas maintain incremental byte counters representing the amount of data emitted and received, respectively. Periodic acknowledgments by replicas confirm the latest offset applied, enabling the master to discard older entries from the replication backlog and to provide precise synchronization points for reconnection.

Chain replication extends the standard master–replica model by organizing replicas in a multi-hop cascade: the master sends write commands to the first replica, which forwards them to the next, continuing down the chain. While this extends write propagation delays, it can reduce the master's networking overhead in large-scale topologies, balancing between latency and scalability. Chain replication also enhances fault tolerance by allowing isolated indirections in case of replica failures, though the complexity of failure recovery increases due to the added dependency chain.

Redis Sentinel and Redis Cluster architectures leverage replication internals for failure recovery and failover. Sentinel monitors replication health by analyzing offsets and ping latencies, promoting replicas to master roles if disconnections or staleness exceed configured thresholds. The replication offset synchronization enables safe master election by ensuring candidates have a synchronized state with a minimum acceptable lag.

In distributed deployments, replication supports multi-master topologies indirectly via client-side sharding or external systems. However, Redis's built-in replication model only supports single-writer scenarios per replication group to maintain data consistency. Replication thus enables data redundancy and read scaling, but complex write conflicts must be managed at the application layer or through clustering techniques.

Finally, replication influences Redis persistence strategies. During full resynchronizations, RDB snapshots are generated without blocking command processing thanks to copy-on-write mechanisms in the forked child process. Command propagation during replication also assists in fast recovery after a crash by replaying the AOF or command logs incrementally on replicas, minimizing data loss windows.

The internals of Redis replication intricately balance consistency, performance, and fault tolerance. The combination of full and partial resynchronization, replication backlogs, incremental offsets, and optional chain replication enables flexible deployment topologies that scale reads, provide data resilience, and facilitate seamless failure recovery. Mastery of these processes is essential for configuring and optimizing Redis in mission-critical distributed applications.

1.5. Sentinel and Automatic Failover Architecture

Redis Sentinel is a specialized distributed system component designed to ensure high availability in Redis deployments by monitoring Redis instances, triggering failover procedures, and facilitating leader election when failures occur. Its architecture embodies a consensus-driven approach that balances responsiveness and consistency through carefully crafted algorithms and communication protocols.

At the core of Redis Sentinel's operation is a network of Sentinel nodes that collectively monitor a Redis primary instance and its replicas. Each Sentinel instance communicates with peers and Redis servers, gathering state information such as node responsiveness, replication offset, and role status. This data is propagated and analyzed to detect failures rapidly and accurately.

Sentinel employs a failure detection mechanism based on two distinct timeout intervals: the *Subjective Down* (SDOWN) and the *Objective Down* (ODOWN) states. When a Sentinel node cannot reach a Redis instance or receives a non-responsive reply, it marks that instance as SDOWN locally. However, to prevent false positives due to transient network anomalies, this state is not sufficient for failover. Instead, the Sentinel instances exchange their observations and coordinate to determine if a majority agree that the node is unreachable, leading to the node being declared ODOWN globally. This global consensus is essential in avoiding split-brain scenarios.

The failover process is triggered only after the ODOWN state is achieved by quorum agreement among the Sentinel quorum. The quorum is defined as a configurable number of Sentinels that must concur about the failure of a monitored Redis primary. This threshold ensures fault tolerance and prevents uncoordinated failovers due to isolated Sentinel failures or inaccurate health assessments.

To establish consensus, Sentinels periodically send and receive hello messages, which carry vital information such as current roles, replication offsets, and Sentinel identities. These messages allow Sentinels to maintain a shared cluster view and to detect discrepancies in the cluster state. A leader election among Sentinels takes place to coordinate the failover procedure; the elected Sentinel assumes the role of failover coordinator.

The leader Sentinel utilizes a distributed voting algorithm inspired by classical consensus protocols, though simplified for Redis's performance constraints. It selects the most suitable replica to promote to primary role based on criteria like replication offset (selecting the replica closest in data freshness to the failed primary), priority settings, and replica health. The leader Sentinel then sends commands to the chosen candidate to execute the failover steps, which include stopping replication, promoting it to primary, and reconfiguring other replicas to follow the new primary.

Handling network partitions presents a critical challenge, as partial visibility among Sentinels or Redis nodes can lead to split-brain conditions. Redis Sentinel addresses this by combining quorum-based agreement with timing constraints. For example, if the Sentinel cluster cannot communicate fully due to network partitions, failover is postponed unless the quorum threshold is met from the majority partition. This approach ensures that only one partition can promote a new leader, preserving data integrity and availability.

In addition to failover coordination, Redis Sentinel maintains continuous monitoring to detect the recovery of failed primaries or any changes in the cluster topology. Once the failed primary is restored, Sentinel can re-integrate it as a replica, ensuring the cluster remains balanced and efficient. This dynamic adaptation mechanism is vital for sustaining long-term cluster health.

Sentinel's design prioritizes eventual consistency of failure states across its distributed nodes. Given the asynchronous nature of the network and message delays, each Sentinel maintains its own view of instance states, gradually converging as messages propagate. Hence, Sentinel avoids immediate, potentially erroneous failovers when partial outages or slow responses occur. Instead, it waits until a strong consensus materializes, balancing availability with correctness.

An overview of the communication pattern is as follows:

- Each Sentinel periodically queries monitored Redis nodes using `PING` and assesses response times.

- Sentinels broadcast `hello` messages to share their current view of the cluster's state.

- Upon detecting a SDOWN, Sentinels exchange votes to determine ODOWN status.

- Once ODOWN is confirmed by quorum, the leader Sentinel initiates failover.

- Commands to change roles and reconfigure replication are sent directly to the Redis nodes.

```
if (sentinel.reportsDown(primary) >= quorum) and
   (not failoverInProgress):
   leader = electLeader(sentinels)
   if (self == leader):
       candidate = selectBestReplica()
```

```
promoteToPrimary(candidate)
reconfigureReplicas(candidate)
```

Fault tolerance is further reinforced by Sentinel's ability to handle multiple simultaneous failures and network instability. By requiring a majority consensus, Sentinel reduces the risk that network partitions trigger split-brain failovers. However, the algorithm relies on timely and reliable communication among Sentinels, necessitating careful network configuration to minimize packet loss and latency.

Redis Sentinel integrates distributed consensus, failure detection, and leader election into a cohesive system that automates Redis failover. Its quorum-based algorithms and continuous state sharing allow it to maintain cluster availability and consistency even under adverse conditions, reflecting a pragmatic trade-off between complexity, reliability, and performance within in-memory data storage environments.

1.6. Cluster Mode and Partitioning

Redis Cluster is a distributed implementation of Redis designed to provide horizontal scaling and high availability by automatically partitioning data across multiple nodes. Its architecture fundamentally revolves around data partitioning through hash slots, dynamic slot assignment, and inter-node communication protocols to maintain consistency and fault tolerance in the cluster.

At the core of Redis Cluster's data distribution mechanism lies the concept of *hash slots*. The cluster keyspace is logically split into 16,384 hash slots, numbered from 0 to 16,383. Each key stored in the cluster is assigned to a slot based on a CRC16 checksum of the key modulo 16,384:

$$\text{slot}(key) = \text{CRC16}(key) \bmod 16384$$

This deterministic hashing ensures that a given key always maps to the same slot, enabling predictable routing within the cluster. Each node in the cluster is responsible for a non-overlapping subset of these slots. The partitioning by hash slots abstracts physical node distribution, effectively implementing a distributed hash table (DHT) that balances data among nodes.

Slot assignment to nodes occurs during cluster bootstrapping. When initializing a cluster, a set of nodes elect one primary node as a *master* and assign hash slots among them, attempting an even distribution of the 16,384 slots to optimize load balancing. The assignment is stored persistently on each node to maintain synchronization. Slave nodes replicate data from their respective masters and serve as failover targets. The cluster configuration, including slot-to-node mappings and replication relationships, is propagated via a gossip protocol to ensure cluster-wide consistency.

Inter-node communication in Redis Cluster hinges on a binary, TCP-based protocol distinct from the standard Redis client-server protocol. Nodes communicate using a gossip-like exchange of state information and cluster messages such as PINGs, PONGs, and FAIL notifications. Each node maintains a cluster state table describing the status of every known node: its unique ID, IP address, port, role (master/slave), and current state. This exchange detects failures and topology changes dynamically.

Cluster bootstrapping initiates by joining a subset of nodes through the cluster meet command, which triggers a handshake and the beginning of gossip exchanges. Nodes validate configuration consistency through cluster info and cluster nodes commands, allowing operators to verify the cluster layout programmatically. Slots can be manually reassigned using commands like cluster setslot, cluster addslots, and cluster delslots to accommodate scaling operations or recover from node failures.

Failure detection in Redis Cluster is decentralized and employs a combination of direct and indirect exchanges. Each node periodically sends PING messages to neighbors. If a node does not respond within a timeout, indirect PINGs are issued via other nodes to confirm failure. A node is marked as *fail* after receiving sufficient confirmation from a quorum of nodes, and the cluster enters a failover process. The failover involves promoting a slave node to master status for the affected hash slots, maintaining data availability with minimal disruption.

The transparent sharding mechanism supported by Redis Cluster abstracts the complexities of distributed storage from clients. Client connections route commands to the appropriate node based on the key's hash slot. If a client attempts to access a key at a node that no longer holds the slot (due to slot migration during rebalancing or failover), the node responds with a MOVED redirection message, instructing the client to retry the command at the correct node. This dynamic discovery and rerouting enable seamless horizontal scaling without requiring the client to manage partition details.

Partitioning via hash slots inherently provides fault isolation. When a node fails or becomes unreachable, only the hash slots owned by that node are affected. The rest of the cluster remains operational and can continue serving requests. This containment limits the blast radius of failures, enabling Redis Cluster to achieve high availability without sacrificing performance or consistency guarantees within each partition.

Redis Cluster's architecture balances efficiency, scalability, and resiliency through its hash slot-based partitioning, meticulous slot assignment, and robust inter-node communication. Its decentralized failure detection and transparent sharding mechanisms collectively ensure that scaling horizontally and isolating faults operate seamlessly in production environments.

1.7. Event Notification and Pub/Sub System

Redis offers robust event notification and publish/subscribe (pub-/sub) capabilities that empower developers to design scalable, loosely coupled distributed systems. These features facilitate asynchronous communication between system components, enabling real-time data propagation and event-driven architectures without tight integration.

At its core, the Redis pub/sub model operates on a messaging paradigm where clients can publish messages to named channels without knowledge of subscribers, and multiple subscribers can listen to these channels to receive messages of interest. The design follows a many-to-many relationship, supporting multiple publishers and multiple subscribers per channel. This abstraction significantly decouples producers and consumers, promoting modularity and scalability in distributed environments.

Redis implements pub/sub through the PUBLISH and SUBSCRIBE commands. When a client issues a PUBLISH command to a given channel, Redis immediately forwards the message to all clients currently subscribed to that channel. Subscribers listen for messages in a blocking manner using the SUBSCRIBE command, which places the client connection into a subscriber mode where it receives messages continually until unsubscribed.

```
SUBSCRIBE channel1 channel2    # Client subscribes to multiple
    channels
PUBLISH channel1 "Hello World" # Client publishes a message to
    channel1
UNSUBSCRIBE channel1           # Stops subscription on channel1
```

The pub/sub system is lightweight and efficient, leveraging Redis' event loop to redispatch messages in-memory with minimal latency. However, the design trade-offs include:

- **No message persistence:** Messages published to a channel are ephemeral and delivered only to subscribers con-

25

nected at the time of publication. Messages are not queued or stored.

- **No guaranteed delivery:** A subscriber disconnected during message delivery or temporarily unavailable will miss published messages.

- **No acknowledgement mechanism:** No native feedback exists to publisher clients indicating whether subscribers received messages.

Because pub/sub messages are transient, Redis pub/sub is best suited for real-time notifications and ephemeral event distribution rather than guaranteed message delivery. For scenarios requiring durable messaging, Redis Streams or external message brokers provide persistence and delivery semantics.

Redis also supports a related mechanism called *keyspace notifications*, which allow clients to subscribe to events triggered by keyspace changes (e.g., key expiration, modification). This feature uses the pub/sub system to broadcast internal Redis events, enabling reactive patterns based on data mutations without polling.

```
CONFIG SET notify-keyspace-events Ex
SUBSCRIBE __keyevent@0__:expired
```

This event notification system can be leveraged to build cache invalidation workflows, trigger asynchronous processing, or monitor system health through Redis.

Delivery Guarantees and Limitations

Given Redis pub/sub's lack of persistence and acknowledgments, it is crucial to assess the implications on system design and incorporate complexity as necessary. The system provides *at-most-once* delivery semantics: messages may be lost if clients disconnect or network issues occur, but rarely duplicated.

To mitigate message loss, typical patterns include:

- **Client replay:** Applications can combine pub/sub to signal the availability of new data and then fetch the full dataset from Redis or persistent storage.

- **Persistent queues for critical messages:** Use Redis Streams or external durable queues alongside pub/sub for asynchronous processing requiring guaranteed delivery.

- **Connection supervision:** Employ client-side logic for reconnection, resubscription, and message recovery upon reconnection.

Decoupling Components with Pub/Sub

Pub/sub enables architectural decoupling by abstracting the communication channels between producers and consumers. This pattern encourages loosely coupled services that independently evolve while maintaining asynchronous interaction.

Common design patterns include:

- **Event-driven workflows:** Services announce state changes or events on channels; downstream components subscribe to relevant events to trigger processing steps asynchronously.

- **Notification systems:** Real-time alerts and notifications propagate through pub/sub without direct integration between senders and receivers.

- **Multiplexed event routing:** Clients subscribe selectively to multiple channels using pattern subscriptions (PSUBSCRIBE), enabling dynamic filtering of messages, which simplifies complex dissemination topologies.

Real-World Use Cases

In practice, Redis pub/sub unlocks significant scalability and flexibility in scenarios such as:

- **Chat applications:** Channels represent chat rooms where users subscribe to receive messages instantaneously. The ephemeral nature suits presence-sensitive features.

- **Live dashboards and real-time analytics:** Backend services publish real-time metrics and events, which dashboards listen to for immediate updates without polling.

- **Microservices coordination:** Microservices communicate events signaling state changes, enabling loosely coupled orchestration and asynchronous event handling without synchronous APIs.

- **IoT data streaming:** IoT devices publish sensor data to channels, and processing units subscribe to filter and aggregate data streams for real-time monitoring.

Pattern subscription extends the system's expressiveness, allowing clients to subscribe to sets of channels matching glob-style patterns, such as subscribing to all channels starting with `device:` in IoT contexts:

```
PSUBSCRIBE device:*
```

Such mechanisms enable hierarchical channel organization, supporting scalable subscription management when channel counts are large or dynamically changing.

Redis's event notification and pub/sub capabilities provide a simple yet powerful foundation for building asynchronous event-driven distributed applications. While the lack of delivery guarantees imposes design constraints, careful architectural patterns can effectively leverage pub/sub to decouple components, reduce complexity, and increase scalability in modern systems.

Chapter 2

Advanced Redis Data Structures

Redis offers far more than simple key-value storage—its sophisticated suite of data structures unlocks powerful new ways to build high-performance applications. This chapter demystifies Redis's advanced data types, revealing how each is engineered for specific access patterns, high scalability, and real-world challenges. Embark on a tour of the internal mechanics, clever use cases, and best practices that make Redis a true data structure powerhouse.

2.1. Strings, Bitmaps, and Bitfields

Redis strings are the fundamental data type underlying many Redis capabilities. Although commonly understood as UTF-8 encoded text, Redis strings are in fact a flexible binary-safe data type capable of storing any sequence of bytes with a maximum length of 512 megabytes. This binary safety permits strings to hold not only textual information but also arbitrary serialized data, including images, compressed objects, or encrypted blobs. The native commands for string manipulation, such as SET, GET, and APPEND, provide efficient and straightforward interfaces to interact with these data sequences.

Beyond simple storage, Redis strings support atomic increment and decrement operations, making them ideal for counters. Commands like INCR, DECR, and their increment-by variants (INCRBY, DECRBY) operate directly on the string values interpreted as integer numbers, facilitating usage patterns for rate limiting, page views counting, or resource tracking. Their atomicity ensures consistent increments in concurrent environments without additional synchronization primitives.

Redis strings also serve as compact flags using individual bits inside a string's bytes. This binary approach to flags allows a single string key to encode multiple on/off states without needing multiple keys. Efficient bitwise operations-accessible through commands such as GETBIT, SETBIT, BITOP, and BITCOUNT-enable manipulating and querying these bit-level flags. For example, a SETBIT command can flip a particular bit index in constant time, allowing developers to track user feature toggles or presence indicators with minimal space overhead.

Extending the concept of bit flags, bitmaps in Redis represent large arrays of bits indexed by integer offsets, where set bits indicate a boolean true state and unset bits indicate false. Bitmaps are particularly useful for efficiently recording presence, state, or membership over large domains without the bloat of storing individual keys or values. For instance, using bitmaps to represent active users by user ID or to implement bloom filters can substantially reduce memory usage compared to alternative data structures.

Redis's bitmap commands work directly over strings with bits treated as an array. Operations such as BITCOUNT provide fast aggregation by counting the number of set bits in a specified range, and BITOP implements bitwise AND, OR, XOR, and NOT across multiple bitmaps, enabling complex set operations for analytics or filtering tasks. The additional command BITPOS can locate the first bit set or clear in a bitmap fragment, facilitating efficient scanning or indexing strategies.

More advanced manipulation of bits beyond simple flags involves bitfields, which group contiguous bits inside a string into numerical subfields of variable bit width. Redis offers the BITFIELD command that can operate on these subfields with commands to get, set, or increment integer values encoded within bitfields, optionally using signed or unsigned interpretation. This capability allows packing multiple small numeric values into a single string key and updating these independent fields atomically and efficiently.

Bitfield operations can be crucial in scenarios requiring compact storage of multiple counters or small state variables. For example, a gaming leaderboard could pack multiple player metrics (scores, levels, achievements) into bitfields, enabling updates and reads with a single network call. The atomicity of BITFIELD ensures consistency in concurrent access without external locking.

The performance merits of bitmaps and bitfields arise from their minimal memory consumption and direct manipulation through bitwise CPU instructions, enabling high throughput with low latency. The compactness achieved by storing many flags or numerical values packed within a single string key reduces the Redis keyspace size and the overhead of managing multiple keys. Additionally, network traffic decreases because fewer commands and smaller serialized payloads are exchanged between clients and Redis servers.

In practice, software architects leverage Redis strings, bitmaps, and bitfields in various patterns: as fine-grained feature flags for A/B testing, presence indicators in social applications, bloom filters for fast membership checks, state retrieval via compact counters in IoT telemetry, and even as lightweight in-memory databases for time series or temporal sequences encoded in bitfields. Understanding the nuances of these capabilities allows practitioners to design systems that capitalize on Redis's internal optimizations and produce highly efficient, scalable solutions.

Careful attention must be paid to the addressing and sizing constraints when using bitmaps and bitfields. Bits are zero-indexed from left to right within a string, and operations outside current string bounds implicitly extend the string, initializing new bits to zero. Although convenient, this behavior can incur additional memory or CPU overhead if used unboundedly. Likewise, when designing bitfields, bit widths and signedness should be chosen to balance compactness and numerical range while avoiding overflow during increments.

Redis strings transcend their apparent simplicity by providing a rich toolkit for representing and manipulating low-level binary data. Bitmaps and bitfields exploit this foundation to offer compact, efficient representations of large arrays of boolean or small-integer states. Mastery of these constructs and their associated commands enables the construction of sophisticated, high-performance data handling paradigms with minimal resource consumption.

2.2. Lists and Streams

Redis provides versatile data structures that facilitate a wide range of use cases, particularly in message queuing, task orchestration, and event-driven systems. Two central primitives in this context are *lists* and *streams*. Both enable ordered sequences of elements but differ significantly in capabilities, internal design, and typical application domains. Understanding their distinctions and complementary use cases is essential for architecting efficient Redis-based pipelines and real-time systems.

Redis lists are implemented as linked lists or quicklists (a hybrid of linked lists and arrays for improved memory efficiency and performance). They provide operations optimized for queue and stack semantics:

- LPUSH and RPUSH: Insert elements on the left (head) or right (tail) of the list.

- LPOP and RPOP: Remove and return elements from the left or right.

- LRANGE: Retrieve a range of elements within the list.

Because of O(1) time complexity for pushing and popping from either end, lists efficiently implement both stacks and queues. For instance, a FIFO queue can be built with RPUSH to enqueue and LPOP to dequeue, or vice versa depending on direction choice. This simplicity supports many classic patterns such as work queues and producer-consumer pipelines.

Atomic operations like BRPOP (blocking pop from right) enable workers to wait for new tasks without polling, providing natural synchronization in distributed environments. Multiple consumers can safely use lists for cooperative task processing, relying on Redis's single-threaded atomicity guarantees.

Lists are particularly suited for transient task queues and job buffers, where message loss is acceptable and order preservation is required but message persistence and replay are not. However, lists lack built-in message acknowledgement, persistence guarantees beyond Redis persistence features, or complex delivery semantics.

Redis streams, introduced in Redis 5.0, augment the capabilities of lists with rich semantics designed for event-sourced and real-time feed architectures. Internally, streams are implemented as log-structured data stores maintained as radix trees of time-ordered entries with unique IDs composed of timestamps and sequence numbers.

Key characteristics that distinguish streams from lists include:

- **Entry IDs**: Each stream entry has a globally unique, ordered ID allowing precise acknowledgment, trimming, and querying by ID ranges.

- **Consumer Groups**: Streams natively support consumer groups, enabling multiple clients to consume entries concurrently while coordinating message delivery. Each consumer tracks its own pending message list and acknowledges processed entries.

- **Message Persistence and Retention**: Streams persist entries until explicitly trimmed (via XTRIM) or evicted, allowing consumers to replay history, process messages at own pace, or recover after crashes.

- **Advanced Delivery Semantics**: Consumers retrieve batches of messages via XREADGROUP, optionally blocking while waiting for new events. The system tracks pending entries per consumer ensuring at-least-once delivery semantics with manual acknowledgment.

- **Range Queries and Event Sourcing**: Applications can query streams by ID ranges (XRANGE) supporting event sourcing patterns, time-windowed analytics, and precisely ordered event reprocessing.

While lists excel as lightweight, high-throughput queues and stacks in scenarios with transient data and basic delivery needs, streams are designed for complex event-driven architectures requiring strong ordering, reliable delivery, and consumer state tracking.

Task Queues and Pipelines

Lists enable simple job pipelines by pushing serialized tasks and popping them atomically for execution. This model suits ephemeral background tasks or throttled workflows where once-consumed messages do not require acknowledgement or guaranteed redelivery.

Event Sourcing and Audit Logs

Streams support the retention of every event with immutable, sequential IDs. This property enables robust event sourcing architectures where system state is reconstructed by replaying the event log with fidelity. Consumer groups allow multiple independent services to consume the same event stream at different rates or epochs.

Real-Time Data Feeds

Streams are ideal for real-time telemetry, analytics, or social feed applications that require ordered delivery guarantees, consumer lag tracking, and message retries in case of failure. The blocking read capabilities with acknowledgment provide natural backpressure handling and fault tolerance.

```
RPUSH task_queue "task1"
RPUSH task_queue "task2"
LPOP task_queue
```

(task1)

```
XADD mystream * sensor-id 1234 temperature 19.8
XREAD COUNT 2 STREAMS mystream 0
```

```
1) 1) "mystream"
   2) 1) 1) "1588153038136-0"
         2) 1) "sensor-id"
            2) "1234"
            3) "temperature"
            4) "19.8"
```

```
XGROUP CREATE mystream mygroup 0
XREADGROUP GROUP mygroup Alice COUNT 1 STREAMS mystream >
XACK mystream mygroup 1588153038136-0
```

The combination of these richer semantics enables Redis streams to solve a broad spectrum of challenges in modern distributed systems, from simple queueing to complex event-driven workflows requiring consistent state replication and failure recovery.

Feature	Lists	Streams
Ordering	FIFO or LIFO (by pushing/popping ends)	Insert-ordered by ID (timestamp+seq)
Delivery Guarantees	Best-effort, no acknowledgements	At-least-once, explicit ACK by consumers
Persistence Model	Volatile unless Redis persistence configured	Persistent with explicit trimming and retention policies
Concurrency	Single consumer or simple multi-consumer with race risks	Native consumer groups with pending message tracking
Query Interfaces	Range by index (LRANGE)	Range queries by ID (XRANGE, XREVRANGE)
Use Cases	Simple queues, stacks, task pipelines	Event sourcing, audit logs, real-time feeds, message buses

Understanding these distinctions enables architects to apply the most suitable Redis primitive according to system requirements, balancing complexity, reliability, and operational semantics in high-throughput, distributed applications.

2.3. Hashes, Sets, and Sorted Sets

Hashes, sets, and sorted sets represent fundamental data structures in modern high-performance databases and in-memory stores, offering distinct primitives for managing grouped attributes, unique membership, and ordered collections, respectively. Each structure is optimized to support diverse access and manipulation patterns relevant to scalable analytics, real-time leaderboards, and complex set-theoretic computations.

Internal Structure of Hashes

Hashes are associative arrays designed to map unique keys to arbitrary values. Internally, hashes utilize either a dynamic array of buckets combined with linked lists or, in high-density cases, open addressing for collision resolution. When collision chaining is employed, each bucket corresponds to a linked list or balanced tree of key-value pairs. Performance-oriented implementations, such as those found in modern key-value stores, adaptively switch between representations to optimize memory layout and access time.

A pivotal aspect lies in the choice of hash functions and resizing algorithms. Universal hash functions minimizing collisions and distributing keys uniformly are imperative for maintaining near-constant-time operations. Resizing typically occurs multiplicatively when load factors exceed threshold values; however, some systems employ incremental or regional rehashing to mitigate latency spikes.

In compact in-memory hashes, values are often stored contiguously with keys using structures akin to hash arrays mapped tries or embedded data encodings. This arrangement enhances cache locality and reduces pointer overhead. Additionally, space optimization is achieved by leveraging variable-length encoding for keys and values when feasible, minimizing fragmentation.

Advanced Hash Manipulation

Advanced hash operations facilitate atomic and composite updates, enabling multi-field transactions crucial in stateful applications. Atomic increments and decrements on numeric fields are supported internally by direct pointer arithmetic without rehashing, preserving throughput in high concurrency environments.

Nested hashes or hashes of hashes support complex domain modeling. Efficient traversal mechanisms rely on custom iterators that inline CPU cache prefetch instructions to reduce latency. Hashes can be scanned incrementally using cursor-based iterators allowing scalable iteration over massive datasets without blocking writes, instrumental in incremental snapshotting and background persistence.

Furthermore, specialized commands for selective deletion, lazy expiration of fields, and partial serialization enable more granular memory management and latency control. Such features are particularly important in use cases where grouped attributes dynamically evolve, for instance, in session stores or user profiles.

Sets for Unique Membership

Sets represent unordered collections of unique elements, focusing on membership queries, additions, and removals with near-constant time complexity. Internally, sets can be implemented via hash tables or bit arrays, depending on element domains and cardinalities.

Large sparse sets utilize hash sets with collision resolution and robust hashing schemes similar to those in standard hashes but optimized for bulk membership checking. For dense integer sets within a known range, bitmaps (bitsets) provide dramatic space savings by encoding membership as bits indexed by element values.

Space Optimization in Sets

When elements are strings or arbitrary binary data, the representation is commonly via a hash table keyed by the serialized representation of elements. Compression techniques such as dictionary coding or prefix compression reduce space requirements, especially when set members share common prefixes.

For very large sets, probabilistic data structures like Bloom filters offer approximate membership queries with tunable false positive rates, trading off accuracy for space and speed. These are often used as fast membership pre-filters before resorting to expensive disk-based lookups.

Set-Based Algorithms for Scalable Analytics

Set operations underpin many analytics algorithms: union, intersection, difference, and symmetric difference compose the core calculus. Efficient implementations rely on sorted internal representations or on exploiting hash-based membership tests.

For example, intersection operations between sets stored as sorted arrays leverage *merge* algorithms with $O(n)$ complexity, where n is the size of the smaller set. When sets are represented as hashes, lookup-based intersection algorithms iterate the smaller set and check membership in the larger set, maintaining linear complexity relative to the smaller operand.

Counting distinct elements can be augmented using HyperLogLog sketches, which provide cardinality estimations with fixed memory usage, facilitating scalable approximate analytics.

Sorted Sets: Combining Uniqueness with Ranking

Sorted sets (or ordered sets) amalgamate the semantics of sets with the additional property of associating each element to a score used for ordering. Internally, sorted sets are typically implemented using a combination of a hash table and a skip list or a balanced tree. The hash table allows $O(1)$ membership and score retrieval, whereas the skip list keeps elements sorted by their score to enable efficient range queries and ranking computations.

Skip lists used in sorted sets maintain multiple levels of forward pointers, providing expected $O(\log n)$ time complexity for insertion, deletion, and range queries, with probabilistic balancing. This hybrid design balances fast lookups with ordered traversals, critical in real-time leaderboard applications.

Advanced Sorted Set Manipulation

Sorted sets offer operations such as range queries by score or rank, rank retrieval, and score increments. Incrementing scores atomically involves unlinking and relinking elements within the skip list to update order without compromising consistency.

To optimize memory, sorted sets employ compact encodings for small scores and short string elements, and avoid redundant storage by sharing pointers between the hash and the skip list. Encoding scores as fixed-point numbers minimizes floating-point overhead while preserving ordering semantics.

Sorted set commands often include intersection and union variants with aggregation functions (sum, min, max), enabling complex cross-set analytics without materializing intermediate sets. These operations are essential in multi-dimensional ranking where multiple scoring criteria are combined.

Applications in Scalable Leaderboards and Analytics

Leaderboards benefit from sorted sets due to efficient insertion, ranking, and trimming of high-score entries. Combined with expiration and partial snapshot capabilities, sorted sets embody dynamic ranking systems with constant update rates.

In analytics pipelines, sorted sets underpin weighted or cumulative scoring and facilitate range queries over ranked results. When coupled with bitmap indexes or secondary indexing structures, sorted sets bring powerful multi-criteria filtering capabilities, which are critical for real-time recommendation engines and anomaly detection.

By integrating optimized in-memory data structures, algorithmic sophistication, and space-efficient encoding, hashes, sets, and sorted sets collectively empower applications to scale both in data volume and operational complexity while maintaining low latency and robust consistency guarantees.

2.4. HyperLogLog and Probabilistic Structures

Cardinality estimation is a fundamental challenge in handling large-scale data, where exact counting is often computationally and memory prohibitive. HyperLogLog (HLL), a probabilistic data structure, addresses this challenge by providing a highly space-efficient algorithm for approximating the number of distinct elements in a multiset. This section examines the principles underlying HyperLogLog, explores its integration in Redis as a built-in feature, and delineates practical considerations to optimize its deployment within distributed systems.

At its core, HyperLogLog leverages hashing and the analysis of leading zero bits within hashed values to estimate cardinalities. Let $h(x)$ denote a uniform hash function generating bit strings, and let $\rho(w)$ represent the position of the leftmost set bit in a binary string w. The algorithm partitions the hash output space into $m = 2^p$ registers, indexed by the first p bits. For each element, the position of the leftmost 1-bit in the remaining (hash length $-p$) bits is recorded in the corresponding register. The maximum observed position in each register serves as an indicator of the density of distinct elements mapping to that register. The algorithm estimates cardinality as

$$E = \alpha_m \cdot m^2 \cdot \left(\sum_{j=1}^{m} 2^{-M[j]} \right)^{-1},$$

where $M[j]$ is the register value and α_m is a bias correction constant dependent on m. This harmonic mean aggregation effectively compensates for the stochasticity inherent in hash collisions. The space complexity is $O(m)$, with m typically chosen between 2^{10} and 2^{16} to balance accuracy and memory.

Redis implements HyperLogLog through the PFADD, PFCOUNT, and PFMERGE commands, abstracting the complexity behind a concise API. Internally, Redis stores HyperLogLog data structures using 12 kB per key by default, providing cardinality estimates with a standard error of approximately 0.81%. This configuration is a tradeoff between precision and memory consumption, making Redis HLL especially attractive in high-throughput environments where the cardinality of large datasets must be approximated rapidly without exact enumeration. The command PFADD adds elements to the HLL, while PFCOUNT returns the estimate of the unique elements observed so far. The PFMERGE command supports the union of multiple HLLs to compute cardinalities across distributed datasets.

An example usage scenario in network monitoring involves estimation of the unique IP addresses observed over a time window. Assuming continuous ingress of billions of packets, exact counting requires maintaining a set of unique IPs, which is infeasible due to memory constraints. Instead, a Redis HyperLogLog can ingest these IPs, providing timely and resource-efficient estimates, enabling anomaly detection or traffic engineering decisions based on cardinality trends.

A key consideration when leveraging HyperLogLog is understanding the probabilistic nature and associated error behavior. Errors arise from hash collisions and limited register size, leading to an expected relative standard error:

$$\text{RSE} \approx \frac{1.04}{\sqrt{m}}.$$

Increasing m improves accuracy but at the cost of additional memory. Moreover, small cardinalities require correction to mitigate estimator bias, and Redis applies empirically derived corrections under the hood for improved estimates at low counts. For critical applications where accuracy is paramount, combining HLL estimates with conventional counting methods during low-cardinality phases can be effective.

When integrating HLL within complex systems, attention must be given to the aggregation and merging operations. Distributed data streams require independent HLLs to be merged without loss of accuracy or excessive overhead. Redis's PFMERGE performs bitwise maximum operations on registers, preserving estimates while enabling scalable parallel computation of cardinalities. In practice, designing the fraction of distinct sets and their temporal decomposition impacts both the accuracy and responsiveness of the estimation output.

Further considerations include the effects of hash function choice

42

and input distribution. A high-quality, uniformly distributed hash function prevents skew that could degrade the statistical assumptions behind HLL. Hash collisions in theory should be rare and have mild effect, but pathological inputs can cause inaccuracies. Thus, deploying cryptographic or well-analyzed non-cryptographic hash functions such as MurmurHash3 or XXHash is advisable.

Probabilistic data structures like HyperLogLog illustrate a broader category of resource-efficient models that approximate set properties with tunable trade-offs. Typically, these structures yield constant or sub-linear memory footprints, enabling large-scale analytics infeasible under exact computation. Combining HLL with complementary probabilistic sketches—for example, Count-Min Sketch for frequency estimation or Bloom filters for membership queries—enables sophisticated query patterns while remaining scalable.

HyperLogLog provides an elegant, practical methodology for approximate counting in data-intensive applications. Redis's native support makes it accessible and performant in distributed systems, contingent on mindful parameter selection and awareness of probabilistic error characteristics. Real-world deployments demonstrate that such probabilistic structures are indispensable in contexts ranging from telemetry, real-time analytics, cybersecurity, to large-scale data warehousing, where resource constraints necessitate approximation without sacrificing operational insights.

2.5. Geospatial Indexes

Redis offers native support for geospatial data, enabling efficient storage, indexing, and querying of geographic locations with minimal overhead. This functionality is built on a specialized data structure that encodes geographic points using geohashes, supporting fast spatial queries such as proximity searches, radius queries, and sorting by distance. These features are essential for modern location-based services and analytics applications, where responsiveness and scalability are vital.

At its core, Redis represents geospatial data as a sorted set, where each member is a unique location identified by a string key, and its score corresponds to the geohash encoding of the location's latitude and longitude. Internally, the geohash is a base32-encoded string that compactly encodes geographic coordinates into a single numeric value. This encoding preserves spatial locality, which allows Redis to leverage sorted set operations for efficient spatial querying.

Storage and Indexing of Locations

The primary Redis command to store geospatial points is GEOADD. It accepts a key for the geo-index, followed by longitude, latitude, and a member name representative of the location. For example, adding a location representing the Empire State Building:

```
GEOADD landmarks -73.9857 40.7484 "EmpireStateBuilding"
```

This command adds the geographic coordinates to the sorted set stored at the key landmarks, with the geohash score automatically computed and maintained by Redis.

Multiple locations can be added atomically, allowing the creation of dense geospatial indexes. Once input, locations can be queried efficiently.

Proximity Searches and Radius Queries

Redis supports several commands to perform spatial queries that retrieve members conditionally based on their distance or position relative to a given point.

The GEORADIUS command finds all members within a circular area defined by a center coordinate and radius. For instance, to find all landmarks within 1 kilometer of Times Square (-73.9851,

44

40.7580):

```
GEORADIUS landmarks -73.9851 40.7580 1 km
```

This query returns members stored inside the *landmarks* geospatial index whose distance from Times Square falls within 1 kilometer. The radius can be specified in meters, kilometers, miles, or feet.

To augment the query, the WITHDIST option instructs Redis to return the distance from the center for each resulting member, facilitating client-side ranking or filtering. For example:

```
GEORADIUS landmarks -73.9851 40.7580 1 km WITHDIST
```

The output includes pairs of members and their associated distances, allowing applications to rank results by proximity.

An advancement over GEORADIUS is the GEOSEARCH command, introduced for flexibility and to discourage legacy command usage. It supports querying with precise bounding boxes instead of circles and allows limiting result counts with COUNT along with sorting options.

Ranking by Distance

Ranking search results by distance is a powerful feature for proximity-based applications. Redis supports this by providing the ASC or DESC options alongside geospatial queries. For example:

```
GEORADIUS landmarks -73.9851 40.7580 5 km WITHDIST ASC
```

This command returns all locations within 5 kilometers sorted in ascending order by their distance to the specified point.

Applications such as ride-sharing, localized advertising, or asset tracking greatly benefit from such ordering, as it facilitates the selection of the nearest resources or places quickly.

Distance Computation

The GEODIST command retrieves the distance between two specified members already stored in a geospatial index. To find the distance between the Empire State Building and Times Square stored
under the same key:

```
GEODIST landmarks "EmpireStateBuilding" "TimesSquare" km
```

This returns a floating-point value representing the kilometers between the two locations, leveraging the same internal geohash and
spherical law of cosines calculations.

Applications in Location-Based Services and Analytics

The built-in geospatial capabilities in Redis are pivotal for real-
time applications that require locality awareness. For example, a
location-based service can swiftly query stores or points of interest
near a user without a heavy geographic information system (GIS)
backend.

In analytics, aggregating geospatial data such as event logs or sensor readings can leverage Redis' radius queries to perform spatial
clustering or heatmap generation efficiently.

The technology also scales horizontally, as Redis clustering supports sharding of geospatial indexes, maintaining high throughput
and low latency for complex queries over large datasets.

Example: Proximity-Based Store Locator

Consider a basic scenario where a mobile application needs to find
all coffee shops within 2 miles of the user's current location (latitude: 37.7749, longitude: -122.4194). The coffee shop locations
are stored in Redis under the key cafes.

```
GEOADD cafes -122.4233 37.7793 "CafeBlueBottle"
GEOADD cafes -122.4141 37.7769 "CafeRitual"
GEOADD cafes -122.4210 37.7689 "CafeFourBarrel"
```

A geospatial search query to list nearby cafes, ordered by proximity,
with distances included:

```
GEORADIUS cafes -122.4194 37.7749 2 mi WITHDIST ASC
```

Typical output from this command could look as follows:

```
1) 1) "CafeRitual"
   2) "0.63"
2) 1) "CafeBlueBottle"
   2) "0.52"
3) 1) "CafeFourBarrel"
   2) "0.72"
```

This output lists cafes within 2 miles, sorted by their distance (in miles) from the user's location, enabling the client to present the closest venues.

Redis' geospatial functionality thus provides a practical and efficient foundation for implementing location-sensitive features, eliminating the need for external GIS databases or complex spatial indexing engines. It is particularly advantageous in scenarios demanding low-latency queries and straightforward integration into existing Redis-backed systems.

2.6. Stream Consumer Groups

Stream consumer groups form a foundational architectural pattern for distributed stream processing, enabling scalable, fault-tolerant consumption of continuous data flows. Their structure supports event-driven systems and message queuing workloads by coordinating multiple consumers that collectively process data from a stream while maintaining consistency and durability guarantees.

At the core, a consumer group comprises multiple instances-consumers-that collaboratively read and process records from one or more streams. Each consumer in the group is assigned a subset of partitions (or shards) from the stream, ensuring a partition-to-consumer mapping that achieves load distribution

47

without overlapping processing. This partition assignment is typically managed by a coordination mechanism that dynamically balances consumers as members join or leave the group, thereby facilitating elasticity.

Partitioned Workload Distribution

A stream is composed of partitions, wherein each partition is a totally ordered, append-only sequence of records. Since each partition preserves message order, consumer groups guarantee strong in-order processing within partitions. By assigning distinct partitions to consumers, the system parallelizes the workload while preserving ordering semantics. This partitioned model allows for horizontal scalability: the number of consumers can be adjusted in response to processing demands by increasing or reducing parallelism, bounded by the number of available partitions.

Partition assignment strategies vary, ranging from static, fixed assignments to dynamic, rebalance-triggered redistribution. The latter relies on a group coordinator which orchestrates membership tracking and partition allocation, balancing factors such as consumer capacity and stream throughput. This coordination is crucial to avoid duplication or message loss during rebalance events caused by failures or scaling activities.

Fault Tolerance and Delivery Guarantees

Consumer groups intrinsically support fault tolerance through consumer failure detection and reassignment of partitions to active group members. When a consumer crashes or becomes unreachable, its assigned partitions are promptly reassigned to other consumers, ensuring continuous processing. This failover process minimizes downtime but incurs a transient rebalance period, during which processing halts for affected partitions.

Durability of processing state is often tied to offset management-the position of the last successfully processed record within a partition. Offsets are maintained externally in a durable, consistent storage system accessible to all consumers in the group. Committing offsets ensures that in the event of consumer restart or reassignment, processing can resume without reprocessing or data loss. Different commit strategies-automatic periodic commits, synchronous commits after processing, or manual commits-balance throughput, latency, and fault tolerance.

Three primary message delivery semantics are supported in this ecosystem:

- *At-most-once*: Records are processed once or possibly discarded during failures. Offset commits happen before processing, minimizing duplicates but risking data loss.

- *At-least-once*: Records are processed at least once, allowing duplicates. Offsets are committed after processing, ensuring no record is skipped but necessitating idempotent processing logic.

- *Exactly-once*: Comprehensive frameworks combine offset transactional commits with atomic processing to guarantee each record is processed precisely once, though at higher system complexity and overhead.

Choosing the appropriate semantics depends on application requirements for accuracy, latency sensitivity, and idempotency capabilities.

Load Balancing and Scalability

Load balancing within consumer groups hinges on the distribution and reassignment of partitions. Adding consumer instances increases parallelism by enabling finer partition granularity allocation. Conversely, reducing consumers leads to aggregation of partitions per consumer. Load skew can arise when partitions have uneven data volumes or processing complexity; mitigation techniques include custom partition assignment algorithms that factor in partition size or processing latency.

Scaling is inherently constrained by the number of partitions in a stream since each partition can be consumed by only one consumer at a time within a group. Planning partition counts to match expected concurrency demands is a critical architectural decision. Over-sharding (excessive partition counts) can introduce management overhead, while under-sharding limits achievable throughput.

Practical Considerations in Balancing Processing and Durability

Stream processing applications utilizing consumer groups must address the trade-offs between throughput, latency, and durability. Frequent offset commits improve recoverability but potentially degrade performance due to I/O overhead. Conversely, delayed commits elevate risk during consumer failure by increasing the duplicated processing window.

Checkpointing state externally, combined with offset commit intervals, can optimize recovery speed while controlling resource consumption. Stateful stream processing systems often integrate consumer groups with snapshots of application state, enabling recovery points that unify message replay with state restoration.

Latency-sensitive applications may favor asynchronous offset commits to avoid blocking on durable storage latency. However, this shifts complexity to the processing logic to handle duplicates and unexpected failures gracefully. Systems implementing exactly-once semantics leverage atomic commit protocols that bind state updates and offset commits, thus providing strong consistency guarantees without manual intervention.

Use Cases in Event-Driven Architectures

Consumer groups are instrumental in event-driven architectures where multiple consumers respond to event streams independently or collaboratively. For instance, microservices can independently subscribe to relevant partitions, ensuring elasticity and fault tolerance while minimizing message duplication. In message queue paradigms, consumer groups provide a publish-subscribe model with balanced load delivery and robust recovery.

When integrated with event sourcing patterns, consumer groups decouple event producers from consumers, allowing independent evolution and scaling. Furthermore, stream processing frameworks augment consumer group patterns with complex event processing, windowing, and aggregation while preserving the fundamental benefits of distributed consumption and fault tolerance.

Stream consumer groups constitute an essential mechanism to realize distributed, scalable, and fault-tolerant stream processing architectures. Their intelligent partition coordination, offset management, and flexible delivery semantics create a powerful abstraction layer that balances processing efficiency and data durability, serving as the backbone for modern event-driven systems.

Chapter 3

Extending Redis: Scripting and Modules

While Redis is renowned for its simplicity and speed, its true power emerges from the ability to extend and customize its behavior. This chapter reveals how developers can harness embedded scripting and the Redis Modules API to push boundaries, automate complex operations, and even craft entirely new data structures within Redis. Venture beyond standard commands to unlock bespoke workflows and tailor Redis for specialized, production-grade use cases.

3.1. Lua Scripting Engine

Redis integrates the Lua scripting language as a powerful extension mechanism that enhances the database's functionality beyond its predefined command set. This integration enables users to execute complex, atomic, server-side operations in a single step, mitigating the need for multiple round-trips and reducing race conditions inherent in concurrent client access. Lua scripts execute within Redis's controlled environment, ensuring deterministic and isolated transaction boundaries.

When a Lua script is invoked, Redis initializes a dedicated execution context where the script runs atomically. All commands within the Lua code are executed sequentially without interleaving other client commands, guaranteeing consistency and isolation. This atomicity is crucial for complex operations such as conditional updates, multi-key transactions, and custom command logic that cannot be composed by traditional Redis commands alone.

The Lua execution environment in Redis exposes a subset of the Lua 5.1 language with a restricted set of libraries to maintain safety and performance. Notable limitations include the absence of I/O and OS libraries to prevent side effects that could compromise server stability or security. The primary interface to Redis commands within Lua is provided by the global `redis.call` and `redis.pcall` functions. The former propagates errors directly to the client, while the latter captures errors as return values, enabling more nuanced error handling strategies within scripts.

Lua scripts running inside Redis operate with a well-defined variable scope. Local variables declared within the script block have lifecycle limited to the script's execution, ensuring no leakage between subsequent script invocations and between different clients. Globals within Lua's environment are sandboxed to prevent persistent mutation. The Redis script environment maintains persistent commands and arguments via special tables, such as `KEYS` and `ARGV`. The `KEYS` table holds keys passed as the first argument to the script, while `ARGV` stores arbitrary additional arguments. This separation promotes best practices by explicitly delineating which keys the script operates upon, facilitating Redis's internal optimizations and providing clarity for script maintainers.

Building reliable and reusable Lua scripts necessitates careful management of variable scope, error handling, and performance considerations. Scripts should minimize the number of Redis calls inside loops to reduce latency and fully exploit atomic execution. When accessing keys, it is essential to pass all keys explicitly in the KEYS array rather than embedding key names statically in the script to leverage Redis's EVALSHA caching mechanism and enable efficient script replication across clustered environments.

Another critical consideration is script idempotence and determinism. Since Redis may automatically re-execute Lua scripts during replication or failover, scripts should avoid non-deterministic functions or side effects external to Redis. Additionally, whenever possible, scripts should use redis.pcall to handle run-time errors gracefully and return structured error information to clients, instead of failing silently or aborting execution.

For example, consider a use case where multiple keys must be conditionally incremented based on the value of another key atomically. Implementing this logic with built-in commands would require multiple round trips and possibly race conditions. Using Redis Lua scripting, the entire logic can be encapsulated in a single script:

```
local threshold = tonumber(ARGV[1])
local currentValue = tonumber(redis.call('GET', KEYS[1]))

if currentValue and currentValue < threshold then
    for i = 2, #KEYS do
        redis.call('INCR', KEYS[i])
    end
    return {ok = "Incremented keys"}
else
    return {err = "Threshold not met or key missing"}
end
```

This script receives a threshold as an argument and a list of keys, queries the first key's value, and increments the remaining keys only if the condition is true, all as a single atomic operation.

To facilitate script reuse and efficient deployment, Redis supports a caching mechanism based on the SHA1 digest of script content. After the first submission via the EVAL command, subsequent invocations can be done with EVALSHA, which reduces parsing overhead and network traffic. Practitioners are advised to distribute scripts with version control and pre-calculate SHA1 hashes to integrate smoothly with Redis client libraries.

Finally, testing and debugging Lua scripts in Redis requires strategies tailored to its embedded context. Developers typically begin by invoking the script via EVAL or the Redis CLI, carefully inspecting return values and error messages. Since the environment restricts some Lua standard libraries, comprehensive unit testing against a controlled Redis instance or within mock environments is recommended to assert functional correctness and performance characteristics.

Redis's Lua scripting engine constitutes a robust, embedded domain-specific language that empowers intricate transactional logic, atomic multi-key operations, and tailored command sequences within the database server itself. Mastery of the Lua environment-including understanding of script scope, argument passing conventions, and best practices for error management-equips developers to extend Redis far beyond its baseline capabilities while maintaining consistency, efficiency, and reliability.

3.2. Transaction Semantics and Pipelining

Redis offers a set of commands that allow client applications to implement transactional semantics and achieve atomicity in a controlled manner. The foundational commands WATCH, MULTI, EXEC, and DISCARD provide a framework for optimistic concurrency control and grouped execution of commands. This approach enables clients to build strong consistency guarantees atop Redis's high-performance single-threaded engine.

The WATCH command acts as an optimistic locking mechanism. By specifying one or more keys with WATCH, the client informs Redis to monitor these keys for any modifications by other clients. If any watched key is altered before the transaction's execution, the transaction will be aborted to prevent race conditions. This ensures that the client operates on a consistent view of the data without requiring explicit locks, thus promoting concurrency. Upon issuing WATCH on specific keys, subsequent commands are sent within a transaction block initiated by MULTI.

The MULTI command signals the start of a transaction block. Commands sent after MULTI are not executed immediately but queued within Redis. Redis acknowledges each enqueued command with an OK response, confirming that the command has been queued successfully. This queuing mechanism allows clients to assemble a batch of commands for atomic execution. The actual execution occurs upon issuing the EXEC command, which triggers all queued commands to be executed in sequence as a single atomic unit. The entire transaction either completes successfully or is discarded if any error or conflict is detected, thus avoiding partial updates.

Should the client decide to abort the transaction before execution, the DISCARD command clears the queue of pending commands and relinquishes any watches set with WATCH. This command is essential for error handling or conditional logic where the client detects that the operation no longer needs to complete atomically.

The optimistic concurrency model enabled by WATCH leverages the fact that conflicts are often rare in concurrent scenarios. Clients attempt to execute transactional operations without pessimistic locking, resulting in reduced latency and higher throughput. However, if a conflict is detected at the time of EXEC, Redis returns a null reply (specifically, null multi-bulk in the Redis protocol) to indicate the transaction was aborted, allowing the client to retry if necessary. This pattern suits workloads with low contention but demanding consistency requirements.

```
WATCH account:12345:balance
MULTI
DECRBY account:12345:balance 100
```

```
INCRBY account:12345:pending 100
EXEC
```

If the balance key is modified by another client between WATCH and EXEC, the transaction will abort and the client will need to reissue the commands or handle the conflict.

Separately, pipelining in Redis is a performance optimization technique for network efficiency during repeated or bulk operations. In a traditional request-response cycle, each command requires a round trip between the client and server, incurring network latency and reducing command throughput. Pipelining enables clients to send multiple commands to the server without waiting for individual responses. Redis processes all commands sequentially and returns their replies in order.

By batching multiple commands in a single network round trip, pipelining minimizes the overhead associated with latency and socket communication. This is particularly valuable when executing a large number of independent commands, such as inserting multiple keys or retrieving ranges in sorted sets. The server's single-threaded architecture ensures commands are processed in submission order, preserving consistency while maximizing throughput.

```
MULTI
SET key1 value1
SET key2 value2
GET key1
GET key2
EXEC
```

While the above example uses MULTI and EXEC to treat commands as one atomic transaction, pipelining does not require transactions. A client may simply write the commands back-to-back to the Redis socket and then read multiple responses after all commands are sent:

```
for cmd in commands:
    socket.send(serialize(cmd))
for _ in commands:
```

```
response = socket.recv()
process(response)
```

This reduces multiple network round trips to a single combined transfer for a batch of commands.

While transactions using MULTI/EXEC guarantee atomicity, pipelining focuses purely on minimizing network latency without providing atomicity. The two concepts are orthogonal but frequently combined for maximal efficiency in client implementations.

Redis's transaction commands provide a controlled, optimistic concurrency model enabling atomic execution of multi-command sequences, suitable for critical operations requiring consistency guarantees. Pipelining complements this by reducing network overhead for command execution, significantly increasing performance for repeated or bulk command scenarios. Understanding and leveraging both paradigms is essential for designing high-throughput, consistent Redis-backed applications.

3.3. Redis Modules API

The Redis Modules API provides a comprehensive interface for extending Redis by writing native C modules. This extension mechanism allows developers to introduce new data types, commands, and behaviors that integrate seamlessly with the Redis core, thereby enhancing functionality while preserving the performance and robustness Redis is known for. The API is designed to ensure safe interaction with the server, proper resource management, and compatibility with Redis's event-driven, single-threaded architecture.

Each Redis module must implement an initialization function named RedisModule_Init, which is called when the module is loaded. This function is responsible for registering new commands and data types, configuring module-level settings, and performing any necessary startup routines. Its prototype is:

```
int RedisModule_Init(RedisModuleCtx *ctx, const char *name, int
    ver, int apiver);
```

where ctx is the context pointer provided by Redis, name is the module's name, ver the module version, and apiver the Redis Modules API version supported. The function returns REDISMODULE_OK upon success or REDISMODULE_ERR on failure, ensuring that the server can handle the load outcome appropriately.

Besides initialization, modules can define an optional cleanup routine invoked during server shutdown, facilitating graceful deallocation of global resources. This lifecycle management aids in maintaining Redis's stability and preventing memory leaks.

A fundamental aspect of module development lies in manipulating keys—the primary data entities within Redis. The API exposes commands to open keys with specific access modes, primarily read or write, guaranteeing atomicity and thread safety compatible with Redis's single-threaded design.

Key handles are retrieved by invoking:

```
RedisModuleKey *RedisModule_OpenKey(RedisModuleCtx *ctx,
    RedisModuleString *keyname, int mode);
```

where mode can be REDISMODULE_READ or REDISMODULE_WRITE. The returned pointer facilitates further operations like type checking, value retrieval, modification, and closing the key.

Modules must check the key's existing type using:

```
int RedisModule_KeyType(RedisModuleKey *key);
```

to ensure compatibility with their internal data format, preventing key corruption and maintaining data integrity across Redis commands.

Access to key values is done through custom functions depending on the module's own data types, often interacting with Redis's own in-memory structures. Both expiration times and persistence states can be queried and modified through dedicated API calls, enabling modules to participate fully in Redis's eviction and persistence mechanisms.

Defining new commands is central to module development and is accomplished via the following API call within RedisModule_Init:

```
int RedisModule_CreateCommand(RedisModuleCtx *ctx, const char *
    name,
                            RedisModuleCmdFunc cmdfunc, const
    char *strflags,
                            int firstkey, int lastkey, int
    keystep);
```

Here, name is the command identifier exposed to clients, and cmdfunc is the C function implementing the command logic. The strflags argument specifies command properties, such as whether it is read-only ("readonly"), write-affecting ("write"), or blocking ("blocking").

Key position arguments (firstkey, lastkey, keystep) optimize Redis's ability to efficiently route commands in a clustered environment. For example, commands operating on a single key typically specify firstkey and lastkey as the same positional index, and keystep as 1.

Careful adherence to these parameters allows Redis to maintain consistency and optimize command execution, especially critical in distributed deployments.

Robust error handling is indispensable for safe module development. The API provides facilities to generate standard Redis replies, error messages, and status codes. The command implementation function uses the context to send replies back to the client:

```
void RedisModule_ReplyWithError(RedisModuleCtx *ctx, const char *
    err);
void RedisModule_ReplyWithSimpleString(RedisModuleCtx *ctx, const
    char *msg);
```

```
void RedisModule_ReplyWithLongLong(RedisModuleCtx *ctx, long long
    ll);
void RedisModule_ReplyWithArray(RedisModuleCtx *ctx, size_t len);
```

Through these calls, modules can return custom error messages while conforming to Redis's protocol syntax. Errors should use well-recognized patterns such as "ERR" prefixes, facilitating client-side error handling and monitoring.

Additionally, command handlers must return status codes from {REDISMODULE_OK, REDISMODULE_ERR} to indicate execution success or failure. Proper error propagation ensures that malformed or invalid operations do not lead to undefined server states.

Consider a module exposing a counter.incr command that increments a stored integer value atomically:

```
int CounterIncr_RedisCommand(RedisModuleCtx *ctx,
    RedisModuleString **argv, int argc) {
    if (argc != 2) return RedisModule_WrongArity(ctx);

    RedisModuleKey *key = RedisModule_OpenKey(ctx, argv[1],
    REDISMODULE_WRITE);
    if (RedisModule_KeyType(key) != REDISMODULE_KEYTYPE_EMPTY &&
        RedisModule_KeyType(key) != REDISMODULE_KEYTYPE_STRING) {
        RedisModule_ReplyWithError(ctx, "ERR wrong key type");
        return REDISMODULE_ERR;
    }

    long long value = 0;
    if (RedisModule_KeyType(key) != REDISMODULE_KEYTYPE_EMPTY) {
        RedisModule_StringToLongLong(RedisModule_StringDMA(key,
    NULL, REDISMODULE_READ), &value);
    }

    value++;
    RedisModule_StringSet(key,
    RedisModule_CreateStringFromLongLong(ctx, value));
    RedisModule_ReplyWithLongLong(ctx, value);

    return REDISMODULE_OK;
}
```

This example illustrates essential API usage patterns: opening keys with correct access modes, validating types, manipulating internal values safely, replying with appropriate data types, and managing error conditions.

- **Resource Management:** Always close keys and free dynamically allocated objects to prevent memory leaks. Use the lifecycle hooks for cleanup.

- **Type Safety:** Verify key types before modification. Consider defining custom data types with the API if needing complex structures.

- **Concurrency Considerations:** Although Redis processes commands sequentially, modules must avoid actions that could block the main thread to maintain responsiveness.

- **Command Flag Accuracy:** Correctly mark commands as read-only, write, or blocking for predictable server behavior, client compatibility, and cluster support.

- **Error Transparency:** Provide meaningful error messages with standard prefixes to aid clients in handling failures gracefully.

The Redis Modules API empowers advanced customization of Redis, enabling the construction of specialized commands and data structures while preserving the server's reliability and efficiency. Mastery of its lifecycle, key handling, command registration, and error mechanisms is essential for building robust, maintainable modules that integrate cleanly within Redis's ecosystem.

3.4. Custom Data Structures in Modules

Redis modules extend the server's capabilities by enabling the definition and implementation of custom data types, also known as module data types. These data types equate to first-class citizens within Redis, allowing seamless integration with core commands, persistence mechanisms, and memory management. Unlike primitive types such as strings or hashes, custom data structures can encapsulate complex behaviors and application-specific semantics not supported natively. This section explicates the systematic approach to designing and implementing custom data types within Redis modules, emphasizing type registration, persistence integration, and efficient memory handling.

The cornerstone of introducing a custom data structure in a Redis module is its registration with the Redis server. This process delivers essential metadata and function pointers to orchestrate serialization, deserialization, memory cleanup, and command interactions.

Registration is performed through the API function `RedisModule_CreateDataType`, which requires the module to specify:

- **Type name:** A unique 9-character string identifier, e.g., `"mymodule_t"`, ensuring no collisions with existing data types.

- **Encoding version:** An integer defining the version of the type encoding, facilitating forward compatibility and versioned persistence migrations.

- **Type methods:** A structure bundling callbacks for memory management, serialization (RDB and AOF), and debugging.

An outline to register a type assumes a modular lifecycle:

```
static RedisModuleType *MyType = NULL;

static RedisModuleTypeMethods MyTypeMethods = {
    .version = REDISMODULE_TYPE_METHOD_VERSION,
    .rdb_load = MyType_RdbLoad,
    .rdb_save = MyType_RdbSave,
    .aof_rewrite = MyType_AofRewrite,
    .mem_usage = MyType_MemUsage,
    .free = MyType_Free,
    .digest = MyType_Digest
```

```
};

int RedisModule_OnLoad(RedisModuleCtx *ctx, RedisModuleString **
    argv, int argc) {
    if (RedisModule_Init(ctx, "mymodule", 1, REDISMODULE_APIVER_1
    ) == REDISMODULE_ERR)
        return REDISMODULE_ERR;

    MyType = RedisModule_CreateDataType(ctx, "mymodule_t", 0, &
    MyTypeMethods);
    if (MyType == NULL) return REDISMODULE_ERR;

    // Additional command registration here

    return REDISMODULE_OK;
}
```

The implementations of the callbacks such as MyType_RdbLoad and
MyType_Free directly control persistence and memory cleanup.
This design grants the module developer full authority over data
lifecycle within Redis.

Persistent storage integration is crucial for custom data types to
ensure durability across server restarts and replication. Redis supports two persistence approaches: RDB snapshotting and AOF
(Append Only File) command log replay. Custom data types must
implement appropriate serialization and deserialization to participate in both.

RDB Serialization and Deserialization

The rdb_save and rdb_load callbacks must marshal the data structure into a format compatible with the Redis RDB binary encoding. Typically, modules serialize all critical fields using the Redis-
Module_Save* and RedisModule_Load* API functions, matching
primitive Redis types and arrays to ensure compact storage.

A precise serialization preserves the internal invariants of the data
structure. For example, consider a custom priority queue structure:

```
int MyType_RdbSave(RedisModuleIO *rdb, void *value) {
    MyPriorityQueue *pq = value;
    RedisModule_SaveUnsigned(rdb, pq->size);
```

65

```
    for (int i = 0; i < pq->size; i++) {
        RedisModule_SaveStringBuffer(rdb, pq->elements[i].key, pq
    ->elements[i].keyLen);
        RedisModule_SaveDouble(rdb, pq->elements[i].priority);
    }
    return REDISMODULE_OK;
}
```

```
void *MyType_RdbLoad(RedisModuleIO *rdb, int encver) {
    if (encver != 0) return NULL; % Unsupported version
    MyPriorityQueue *pq = MyPriorityQueue_Create();
    size_t len = RedisModule_LoadUnsigned(rdb);
    for (size_t i = 0; i < len; i++) {
        char *key;
        size_t keyLen;
        key = RedisModule_LoadStringBuffer(rdb, &keyLen);
        double priority = RedisModule_LoadDouble(rdb);
        MyPriorityQueue_Insert(pq, key, keyLen, priority);
        RedisModule_Free(key);
    }
    return pq;
}
```

Strict version checks and precise field order during load/save are
critical to avoid data corruption or desynchronization across Redis
versions.

AOF Rewrite

The `aof_rewrite` callback reconstructs the commands that will re-
produce the data structure's contents when replayed. This mechanism is essential for compatibility with command logging and replication.

Commands emitted typically mirror the module's public interface
commands, e.g., MYTYPE.ADD or MYTYPE.REMOVE. Providing an efficient, minimal set of commands during AOF rewrite reduces log
size and speeds recovery.

Memory management for custom data structures requires implementing a `free` callback wherein all resources, including nested
allocations and auxiliary buffers, are released appropriately to prevent leaks.

Redis modules employ RedisModule_Alloc, RedisModule_Free, and related APIs instead of standard `malloc/free` to maintain compatibility with Redis's internal memory tracking and reporting.

```
void MyType_Free(void *value) {
    MyPriorityQueue *pq = value;
    for (int i = 0; i < pq->size; i++) {
        RedisModule_Free(pq->elements[i].key);
    }
    RedisModule_Free(pq->elements);
    RedisModule_Free(pq);
}
```

Another auxiliary method is `mem_usage`, which returns the estimated memory consumption of the data structure. This information improves Redis's internal statistics and memory eviction behavior.

Native Redis data types excel at simple key-value and collection paradigms but lack expressive structures for domain-specific tasks. Modules can meet these needs by introducing bespoke abstractions:

- **Priority Queues and Heaps:** Efficiently scheduling jobs or events sorted by priority, impossible with native sorted sets when performance demands custom comparison logic or additional attributes.

- **Graphs and Trees:** Applications requiring adjacency lists, traversal state, or hierarchical relationships use modules to encapsulate graph algorithms and structural integrity.

- **Compressed or Trie-based Indexes:** Advanced search or autocomplete applications incorporate compressed tries or other indexes to offer near-real-time querying, which native string or hash structures cannot emulate.

These data structures integrate seamlessly with Redis commands,

Lua scripting, and replication, providing a transparent and performant extension to the core feature set.

By treating custom data types as first-class entities, modules advance Redis beyond a mere key-value store into a versatile, domain-adaptable data platform. The combination of explicit lifecycle management, robust persistence interfaces, and memory control facilitates maintaining data integrity and operational robustness at scale.

3.5. Sandboxing and Security in Scripting

Server-side scripting inherently elevates security risks, especially in environments where scripts can be submitted and executed dynamically. Redis scripting, primarily via Lua, introduces mechanisms designed to mitigate these risks, but a thorough understanding of sandboxing, resource limitation, and attack vectors remains essential for robust deployment.

Redis employs a lightweight sandboxing model for Lua scripts that effectively restricts the execution environment. By design, scripts run within the Redis server process with a dedicated Lua interpreter instance stripped of all external libraries except for the essential Redis API commands. This sandbox prevents file system access, networking, and operating system calls from within scripts, thereby confining script capabilities strictly to Redis internal commands. The absence of arbitrary external access significantly reduces the attack surface, forbidding operations that could otherwise compromise the host system or data outside Redis.

Resource limitation is a paramount concern given that long-running or infinite loops within scripts could exhaust server CPU time and degrade service availability. Redis introduces several controls to address this. First, there is a built-in script time limit, configurable via the `lua-time-limit` setting, which aborts scripts exceeding a defined CPU time threshold (defaulting to 5 seconds). This ensures that any runaway script is forcibly terminated, preserving overall system responsiveness. Additionally, the single-threaded nature of the Redis server implicitly serializes script execution, preventing concurrent resource contention but also necessitating strict attention to script efficiency.

Memory consumption within scripts is constrained both implicitly and explicitly. The Lua environment maintains local memory for script variables, but Redis restricts the command replies and key metadata that scripts can alter or return. Scripts that generate excessively large multi-bulk replies or attempt to access large datasets incur penalties because their execution time and memory footprint increase, potentially triggering the time limit or causing latency spikes. Careful script design, including bounded iteration and minimal data return, is critical to avoid denial-of-service (DoS) scenarios.

To prevent abuse, Redis discards the use of potentially dangerous Lua functions, restricting the scripting language to a deterministic subset. For example, functions for dynamic code loading, operating system interaction, or random number generation beyond a deterministic seed are banned or carefully controlled. This limits unpredictability and side effects, which can be exploited for attacks such as timing analysis or privilege escalation. Moreover, Redis scripts operate without persistence in the Lua state; each script invocation starts with a fresh Lua environment, minimizing state-based attacks and memory leaks.

In multi-tenant environments, where multiple users or client applications may submit scripts, enforcing isolation and safety is even more challenging. Native Redis scripting does not provide user identity or permission checks for scripts; all scripts run with the connected client's privileges. Consequently, best practices involve implementing application-layer controls to validate, sanitize, and securely manage submitted scripts before execution. One common approach is to pre-load only vetted, parameterized Lua scripts into Redis, avoiding arbitrary script ingestion. Clients then execute these pre-approved scripts using SHA hashes, preventing injection or execution of unauthorized code.

Complementing this, resource consumption policies can be enforced externally by monitoring execution times and issuing alerts or termination commands for misbehaving clients. Rate limiting and usage quotas reduce the risk that a compromised tenant can degrade service quality or access data beyond their scope. Where more granular access control is required, some architectures employ separate Redis instances or logical databases, combined with application-level authentication and strict network segmentation.

Another technique to enhance security is to limit the Redis command set accessible to scripts by design. Through command renaming or disabling certain potentially harmful commands (e.g., DEBUG, EVALSHA allowing script re-evaluation), administrators can reduce attack vectors. Additionally, specialized Redis modules can be leveraged to create confined scripting capabilities with narrower functional scopes, tailored to specific business needs while reducing exposure.

Redis script sandboxing hinges on isolating the execution environment, restricting system-level side effects, and imposing resource limits to safeguard server integrity. Avoiding vulnerabilities requires conservative script design: constrained access patterns, bounded resource consumption, and strict vetting procedures for script acceptance. For multi-tenant scenarios, combining Redis's built-in controls with comprehensive external governance—pre-approved script sets, client authentication, command restrictions, and monitoring—ensures safe extensibility without compromising security. These layered defenses collectively maintain Redis as a powerful yet secure platform for server-side scripting in demanding environments.

3.6. Performance Considerations for Extensions

Redis is renowned for its exceptional single-threaded performance, driven by a carefully optimized event loop and in-memory data structures. When integrating extensions such as Lua scripting or Redis modules, preserving this performance is paramount. Both scripting and modules introduce custom processing logic that, if not properly managed, can degrade the throughput and latency Redis offers. This section dissects the key performance considerations when incorporating extensions, emphasizing monitoring, profiling, and design patterns that ensure resource-efficient, high-speed operation consistent with Redis's architecture.

Impact of Scripting on Performance

Lua scripts in Redis execute atomically within the server process, blocking other clients until completion. The atomicity guarantees data consistency but increases the risk of latency spikes if scripts run for excessive durations or consume disproportionate CPU resources. Scripts that perform heavy computations or iterate over large datasets should be carefully benchmarked to prevent blocking the event loop.

Execution time of Lua scripts can be monitored using commands such as SCRIPT STATS, introduced in Redis 7.0, which provides metrics about individual scripts' invocation counts and total execution time. Additionally, SLOWLOG entries can reveal problematic scripts by capturing commands and scripts whose execution time exceeds configured thresholds.

Profiling Lua scripts requires instrumenting the code with careful timing or logically decomposing complex operations into smaller scripts or Redis commands. Where possible, leveraging Redis commands optimized for set and hash operations instead of performing equivalent logic within Lua is preferred.

71

Modules and Their Effect on Throughput and Latency

Redis modules extend Redis functionality by hooking into its event loop and command processing. While modules allow complex data types and commands implemented in compiled languages (typically C), they can threaten Redis's performance model if they block or consume excessive CPU cycles.

A critical design constraint for modules is non-blocking execution within the main event loop. Long-running computations or I/O-bound operations must be offloaded to background threads or external workers through the Redis module thread API, or by adopting asynchronous designs. Failure to do so risks increasing request latencies and impacting all connected clients.

Memory management within modules also affects performance; modules should avoid frequent dynamic allocations and deallocations and prefer using Redis's allocator or pre-allocated buffers where possible. Additionally, adherence to Redis's memory policies and keeping memory usage predictable ensures stable performance under load.

Monitoring and Profiling Extensions

Monitoring extension performance involves combining Redis's core diagnostics with extension-specific metrics. INFO sections such as commandstats include latency distributions and invocation counts but cannot capture module-internal metrics unless explicitly programmed.

Modules can be instrumented using Redis statistics APIs, emitting custom statistics visible via commands like MODULE STATS or user-defined statistics commands. Instrumentation should provide latency percentiles, success rates, error counts, and resource usage snapshots.

For Lua scripts, apart from SCRIPT STATS and slowlog entries, wrappers can be developed to record timestamps at script start and end, enabling in-depth analysis. Profiling tools like `perf` or system-level profilers can also elucidate CPU hotspots introduced by modules.

Optimization Strategies and Design Patterns

Maintaining Redis's speed mandates strict control of extension complexity. Recommended design patterns include:

- **Separation of Concerns:** Decompose complex logic into smaller, atomic operations executed by Redis native commands or minimal Lua scripts instead of monolithic scripts or commands.

- **Batching and Pipelines:** Minimize round trips by grouping commands or script calls where feasible. Batching can improve amortized cost per operation while keeping scripts short.

- **Incremental Processing:** For modules, implement incremental command handlers that can be resumed, spreading heavy computations across multiple event-loop iterations to avoid blocking.

- **Resource Limits:** Implement strict execution time or memory usage thresholds for scripts and module commands, aborting or returning errors when limits are exceeded to maintain overall system responsiveness.

- **Asynchronous Execution:** Leverage Redis's thread-safe APIs to offload long-running operations to worker threads, returning results asynchronously to clients, thereby preserving the single-threaded event loop's responsiveness.

- **Cache and Memoization:** Where operations are repeated, use caching techniques to avoid redundant computations inside scripts or modules.

- **Memory-Friendly Data Structures:** Favor compact, efficient data encodings and avoid copying large datasets unnecessarily within custom logic.

Case Study: Optimizing a Lua Script Extension

Consider a Lua script intended to compute aggregations over large sorted sets. A naive implementation iterates over the entire set in a single execution, causing significant latency spikes. A better design partitions the input into chunks processed by successive calls, each processing a fraction of the data and storing intermediate results in Redis keys. A controlling application client invokes these chunked scripts in a pipeline, assembling the final result incrementally while ensuring no single invocation blocks the server excessively.

Summary of Key Metrics to Monitor

- **Script execution time**: Average, maximum, and percentile latencies per script.

- **Module command latency**: Measured via internal instrumentation or commandstats.

- **Memory consumption**: Heap and stack growth attributable to extensions.

- **CPU usage**: Profiled per module or script to detect hotspots.

- **Error and abort counts**: Frequency of extension-executed commands failing or aborting due to resource limits.

Integrating these metrics into operational monitoring enables rapid identification of performance regressions associated with extension logic.

Effectively deploying Redis extensions requires a deep understanding of their impact on the core event loop, memory system, and concurrency model. Through careful design, judicious monitoring, and iterative profiling, both Lua scripting and modules can augment Redis's capabilities without compromising its hallmark performance. Adhering to recommended design patterns-focusing on short execution times, incremental work distribution, and resource constraint enforcements-ensures that extensions maintain Redis's blazing speed and responsiveness.

Chapter 4

Scaling, High Availability, and Disaster Recovery

Mission-critical applications demand databases that scale seamlessly, remain available in the face of faults, and protect data against catastrophic loss. This chapter pulls back the curtain on the practical and architectural patterns that empower Redis to meet these rigorous demands. Learn how Redis clusters grow to handle millions of operations per second, how failover mechanisms keep your data accessible, and how robust disaster recovery shields your business from the unexpected.

4.1. Replicated and Partitioned Topologies

Scaling Redis to accommodate increased workload or improve availability involves leveraging two fundamental architectural patterns: replication and partitioning. These approaches address different dimensions of scalability-replication primarily enhances vertical scaling for read throughput and fault tolerance, while partitioning enables horizontal scaling through data sharding across multiple nodes. Understanding the nuances of these topologies and their trade-offs is critical for designing performant and resilient Redis deployments.

Replication Architecture

Replication in Redis is executed through an asynchronous primary-replica mechanism. A single primary node accepts writes and propagates data to one or more read-only replicas. This architecturally achieves vertical scaling by distributing read operations across the replicas, thereby increasing read throughput and improving availability. Replication also facilitates failover strategies, allowing replicas to be promoted to primary roles in case of failures.

Replication topology can be summarized as follows:

- **Primary-Replica Model**: Writes target the primary, which asynchronously replicates data changes to replicas.

- **Asynchronous Replication**: Replicas lag behind primary updates, with a replication offset indicating delay, which can lead to eventual consistency but not strong consistency.

- **Read Scalability**: Applications can distribute read queries to replicas, easing load on the primary and improving latency and throughput.

- **High Availability**: Failover mechanisms promote replicas to primaries, minimizing downtime.

From a deployment perspective, Redis Sentinel or Redis Cluster provide orchestration layers to automate failover, monitor node health, and reconfigure clients. Sentinel coordinates failover by electing new primaries when the current primary is unreachable, while Redis Cluster integrates replication within a sharded environment.

Trade-offs of Replication

While replication enhances read scalability and availability, it introduces several trade-offs:

- **Eventual Consistency**: Due to asynchronous replication, replicas may serve stale data during replication lag. This affects applications that require strong read-after-write consistency.

- **Write Scalability Limit**: Writes are confined to the primary node, limiting vertical scaling for write-heavy workloads.

- **Failover Complexity**: Automated failover can introduce brief service interruptions during election and reconfiguration phases.

- **Increased Resource Usage**: Maintaining replicas requires additional memory and CPU resources per replica.

Careful calibration of replication factors and heartbeat intervals in Sentinel or Cluster minimizes these trade-offs.

Partitioning and Sharding

Partitioning Redis data across multiple nodes fundamentally enables horizontal scaling, extending both read and write capacities. Unlike replication, which duplicates entire datasets, partitioning divides a single dataset into disjoint subsets or shards. Each shard manages a subset of keys, and collectively the shards represent the entire keyspace.

Redis supports partitioning primarily through Redis Cluster-a native sharding solution that distributes data automatically:

- **Hash Slot Mechanism**: The keyspace is divided into 16,384 hash slots, each assigned to a cluster node. Keys are mapped to slots using a hash function, deterministically routing requests.

- **Distributed Hash Table**: The cluster nodes maintain metadata about slot-node mappings, allowing any client to compute the responsible node without a centralized router.

- **Scalable Writes and Reads**: Writes are distributed among cluster nodes, enabling parallel processing and increased throughput.

- **Replication per Shard**: Each shard can have its own replicas, combining partitioning with replication to ensure availability.

Partitioning transforms Redis into a distributed key-value store supporting larger datasets exceeding a single node's memory limits and higher concurrency.

Trade-offs of Partitioning

Partitioning introduces complexity and operational considerations:

- **Cross-Slot Operations**: Commands involving multiple keys are constrained to keys within the same hash slot, limiting support for multi-key atomic operations. This necessitates careful key design or application-level coordination.

- **Rebalancing Overhead**: Resharding to add or remove nodes requires migrating hash slots and associated data, which can impact cluster performance during migration.

- **Increased Complexity**: Client libraries must handle cluster topology updates and redirections transparently, adding complexity to deployment.

- **Partial Failures**: Node or network failures affect only specific shards, allowing partial availability but complicating consistency guarantees.

These constraints influence topology design, driving choices such as the number of shards, replication factor per shard, and key distribution strategy.

Topology Design Considerations

Architecting a scalable Redis infrastructure requires balancing availability, performance, consistency, and operational complexity. Key considerations include:

- **Workload Characteristics**: Read-heavy workloads benefit more from replication, while write-heavy or very large datasets necessitate partitioning.

- **Consistency Requirements**: Applications with strict consistency demands may need to trade some performance and availability to ensure synchronous replication or use external coordination.

- **Deployment Environment**: Cloud-native deployments leverage managed Redis services with built-in replication and partitioning, while self-managed clusters require explicit topology configuration and monitoring.

- **Failover and Recovery**: Using Redis Sentinel or Redis Cluster's built-in failover capabilities improves resilience but requires validation of failover time impact on SLAs.

- **Monitoring and Observability**: Tracking replication lag, cluster slot allocation, and node health is critical to maintaining a balanced topology.

Hybrid Topologies

In many real-world scenarios, hybrid topologies combining replication and partitioning maximize benefits. Redis Cluster nodes maintain replicas, providing fault tolerance at the shard level. This combined approach scales both horizontally and vertically, enabling robust architectures that handle diverse traffic patterns and failure modes.

Deployment Strategies

Common deployment patterns include:

- **Single Primary with Multiple Replicas**: Simple vertical scaling for read-heavy workloads with availability.

- **Redis Cluster with Replicated Shards**: Distributed, scalable, and fault-tolerant, suitable for large and critical applications.

- **Proxy-Based Partitioning**: External proxy layers implement sharding logic on top of multiple standalone Redis instances; this approach adds operational complexity and latency.

Each strategy must be aligned with operational expertise, latency tolerance, complexity preferences, and expected scaling trajectories.

Replicated and partitioned topologies form the backbone of scalable, resilient Redis architectures. Mastering their mechanisms, trade-offs, and optimal deployment scenarios enables building high-performance distributed key-value stores tuned to specific application demands.

4.2. Redis Cluster Administration

Redis Cluster distributes data across multiple nodes using a fixed hash slot mechanism, where the keyspace is divided into 16,384 hash slots. Each node in the cluster is responsible for a subset of these hash slots. Effective day-to-day administration of a Redis Cluster involves managing these hash slots to maintain performance, ensure data availability, and accommodate changes in workload.

Managing hash slots begins with understanding the cluster's current slot distribution. Using the CLUSTER SLOTS command, administrators can query the cluster to see how slots are allocated among nodes, including masters and replicas. This information is crucial for diagnosing imbalances and planning resharding operations. Imbalances can occur when nodes serve disproportionate numbers of clients or experience uneven data growth, leading to hotspotting or resource exhaustion.

Resharding redistributes hash slots across the cluster to correct imbalances. The process involves migrating keys from source nodes to target nodes while minimizing the impact on availability and performance. Redis provides a built-in tool for resharding through the Redis Cluster Management utility (e.g., redis-cli with the --cluster option) that automates slot migration. The key steps in resharding are:

1. Identify source and destination nodes and the number of slots to move.

2. Put the cluster in a state suitable for migration without disrupting client operations.

3. Migrate keys slot-by-slot, ensuring consistency and atomicity as keys move.

4. Update the cluster configuration to reflect new slot ownership.

A critical aspect of resharding is slot migration's incremental nature, migrating a limited number of slots at a time to avoid overloading network and CPU resources. This reduces downtime and prevents clients from encountering missing keys during migration.

Adding nodes to a Redis Cluster typically follows a procedure beginning with joining a new node as a master or as a replica. The CLUSTER MEET command is used to introduce the node to the cluster, after which resharding can redistribute hash slots to integrate the new node's capacity evenly. When adding replica nodes, the administrator uses CLUSTER REPLICATE to link a replica to its master, providing redundancy and failover capabilities.

Removing nodes involves migrating all hash slots from the node slated for removal to other masters, then using CLUSTER FORGET to remove the node's record from the cluster configuration. Before removal, it is essential to ensure no slots remain assigned to that node. Removing a node without migrating slots can cause data loss and cluster inconsistency. Careful planning is needed to avoid partitioning and maintain cluster quorum.

Safe rebalancing of clusters is foundational to avoiding data loss or service interruptions. A recommended practice is to monitor cluster health continuously with tools such as redis-cli, Redis Sentinel, or third-party monitoring systems capable of tracking node states, slot distribution, and latency metrics. Before initiating rebalancing or node changes, administrators should create a backup of the cluster data, particularly if the cluster is used in production environments.

During rebalancing, the following best practices minimize risks:

- Perform migrations gradually, redistributing slots in small batches.

- Temporarily throttle client loads if possible, reducing the pressure on nodes during slot movement.

- Use replicas to ensure failover capability in case of node failure mid-operation.

- Automate checks for cluster state consistency after each batch migration.

- Schedule maintenance during low-traffic periods to reduce impact.

The `redis-cli --cluster` utility encapsulates many of these precautions, offering interactive commands such as `reshard`, `add-node`, and `del-node` with built-in validation and prompts.

Example commands for adding a new master node and resharding 3000 slots from an existing master to the new node are:

```
redis-cli --cluster add-node 192.168.1.100:6379 192.168.1.50:6379
redis-cli --cluster reshard 192.168.1.50:6379
```

During resharding, administrators are prompted to specify the source node, destination node, and number of slots to move interactively, ensuring deliberate control over the operation.

Ensuring the cluster remains balanced with the appropriate number of replicas for fault tolerance is equally important. Administrators should periodically verify that every master has a replica and that no replicas remain orphaned due to node removals or failures. Replica promotion procedures must be tested and operational to withstand master failures transparently.

In environments with frequent cluster scaling, automation via scripts or orchestration tools integrating Redis cluster commands helps reduce human error and improves consistency. However, administrators must remain vigilant about network partitions and split-brain scenarios, which can compromise cluster integrity.

Effective Redis Cluster administration requires continuous monitoring, controlled management of hash slots through resharding, cautious node addition and removal, and strict adherence to best practices in rebalancing. Leveraging built-in Redis tooling alongside comprehensive operational procedures ensures minimized downtime and resilience against data loss, maintaining reliable high-performance key-value storage across distributed infrastructures.

4.3. Sentinel Best Practices

Redis Sentinel is a resilient system designed to provide high availability for Redis deployments by monitoring Redis instances, performing automatic failovers, and issuing alerts upon failures or state changes. To effectively deploy and configure Redis Sentinel, it is essential to understand its operational mechanisms, potential failure modes, and integration strategies within real-world environments.

A robust Sentinel deployment consists of multiple Sentinel processes distributed across different hosts. This redundancy ensures fault tolerance and consensus-based decision making. A recommended minimum is three Sentinel instances per monitored Redis master to guarantee a quorum during failover decisions. Running fewer than three Sentinels risks inconsistent failover behavior and split-brain scenarios.

Each Sentinel instance requires a configuration file specifying the masters to monitor, quorum size, failover parameters, and notification settings. The key directives include:

```
sentinel monitor <master-name> <ip> <port> <quorum>
sentinel down-after-milliseconds <master-name> <milliseconds>
sentinel failover-timeout <master-name> <milliseconds>
sentinel parallel-syncs <master-name> <count>
```

`sentinel monitor` establishes the master node Sentinel will observe. The quorum value is critical, representing the minimum Sentinel votes required to consider the master unreachable and initiate a failover. Setting quorum to a majority of Sentinel nodes ensures consistent agreement.

`sentinel down-after-milliseconds` controls the detection time before marking a master as subjectively down (SDOWN). Lower values increase sensitivity but may trigger false positives in unstable network conditions. Fine-tuning this parameter requires balancing detection speed and stability.

For failover operations, `sentinel failover-timeout` defines the maximum allowed time to perform a failover, including slave promotion and client notification. `sentinel parallel-syncs` specifies the number of replicas that can be reconfigured simultaneously to replicate from the new master, optimizing replication catch-up speeds.

After configuring Sentinels, they must be launched so they form a consensus cluster. Upon startup, Sentinels exchange hello messages and elect a leader responsible for orchestrating failovers. This Sentinel leader selection is dynamic and relies on majority voting.

Split-brain arises when distinct Sentinel subsets independently elect different masters, causing data divergence. Mitigating split-brain requires careful quorum and network topology planning.

- **Quorum Majority:** Always set the quorum value greater than half the total number of Sentinels. For example, in a 3-Sentinel deployment, quorum should be at least 2.

- **Distribute Sentinels Across Failure Domains:** Run Sentinels in multiple racks, availability zones, or geographic locations. This ensures that a network partition affecting a subset of Sentinels does not cause inconsistent failover decisions elsewhere.

- **Network Stability:** Employ reliable inter-Sentinel communication channels with low latency. Use dedicated networks or VPNs with quality of service (QoS) guarantees to minimize false failure detections.

High-throughput, latency-sensitive environments often require

Sentinel tuning to avoid unnecessary failovers and minimize recovery time.

Adjust Failure Detection Sensitivity The down-after-milliseconds setting should be adapted based on typical network latency and Redis operation response times. In stable internal networks, values of 5,000 ms or lower allow prompt detection. In contrast, in cloud or WAN deployments, values of 10,000 ms or higher reduce failover flapping.

Failover Timeout Operations during failover, such as slave promotion and redirecting clients, must complete before failover-timeout expires. This timeout must exceed the maximum expected synchronization time for slow or large datasets. Monitoring replication backlog size and network performance informs this tuning.

Parallel Synchronization Redis Sentinel allows simultaneous resynchronization of multiple replicas with the new master by configuring parallel-syncs. Setting this to a value larger than 1 accelerates cluster recovery but may increase load on the master during failover.

Sentinel supports hooks for custom alerting workflows integrating with operational monitoring platforms or incident response systems.

```
sentinel notification-script <master-name> /path/to/script.sh
sentinel client-reconfig-script <master-name> /path/to/reconfig.
    sh
```

The notification-script is invoked on events such as master down, failover start, or completion, allowing custom alert dispatch via email, Slack, or PagerDuty integrations. The client-reconfig-script enables client-side reconfiguration, essential for updating application endpoints post-failover.

Successful workflows often involve combining Sentinel event scripts with centralized logging and monitoring frameworks, such

88

as Prometheus with alertmanager, or ELK stacks. Real-time visibility into Sentinel state transitions helps operators respond rapidly to failures and investigate anomalies.

- **Persistent State:** Enable Sentinel's `sentinel announce-ip` and `sentinel announce-port` directives in containerized or dynamic IP environments to ensure Sentinels correctly advertise their network addresses.

- **Backup Policies:** Despite Sentinel's failover capabilities, integrate regular backup processes since failover promotes instantaneous switchover but does not substitute for point-in-time recovery strategies.

- **Testing Failover Procedures:** Conduct controlled failover drills to verify that Sentinel correctly triggers failover and that application clients seamlessly follow the new master without manual intervention.

- **Avoid Single Points of Failure (SPOF):** Ensure that Redis replicas are distributed across different hosts or zones to prevent correlated failures taking multiple nodes offline along with the master.

Comprehensive Sentinel deployments that balance quorum configuration, network reliability, failover parameter tuning, and alerting integration significantly improve Redis system availability and operational resilience. Following these best practices enables consistent master election, rapid recovery, and minimal service disruption under fault conditions.

4.4. Geo-Distributed Redis Deployments

The deployment of Redis across multiple geographically dispersed data centers or cloud regions introduces a unique set of challenges

primarily centered around latency, data consistency, fault tolerance, and operational complexity. Unlike a local or single-region
setup, geo-distributed Redis environments must accommodate the
physical and network distance separating nodes, necessitating specialized replication strategies and architectural adjustments.

At the core, Redis was designed as a high-performance, single-
threaded, in-memory key-value store optimized for low-latency access. When the deployment domain expands beyond a single data
center, the network delays inherent in cross-region communication threaten Redis's responsiveness. Mitigating these challenges
requires carefully designed replication mechanisms tailored to balance consistency, availability, and latency constraints.

Cross-Region Replication Techniques

Traditional Redis replication is based on a primary-replica model
with asynchronous replication. The primary node handles write
operations, propagating changes to replicas via a replication log.
This works efficiently within a single data center but is insufficient
for geo-distribution without modifications. Given network latencies that can reach tens or hundreds of milliseconds between regions, naïve asynchronous replication risks exposing stale data to
users and lagging replicas that degrade read locality guarantees.

To address this, geo-distributed Redis deployments often leverage
semi-synchronous or hybrid replication techniques:

- **Asynchronous replication with dedicated read replicas per region:** This approach deploys one primary Redis
  instance in a single region handling writes, while replicas
  in other regions subscribe asynchronously to updates. Although write latency remains low at the primary, read requests targeting remote regions may observe eventual consistency and stale data. This strategy suits applications tolerant
  to relaxed consistency and prioritizes global read scalability
  with write centralization.

- **Active-Active replication:** Utilizing Redis Enterprise modules or third-party solutions like Redis Raft, active-active configurations enable multiple primaries across regions. Data is synchronized using conflict-free replicated data types (CRDTs) or consensus protocols, allowing writes to occur in any region with eventual reconciliation. Active-active deployments dramatically reduce write latency and improve availability but require complex convergence management and tolerate weak or eventual consistency semantics.

- **Partial or selective replication:** A hybrid approach only replicates subsets or partitions of data across regions. Applications segment Redis keyspaces by geographic boundaries or data relevance, minimizing cross-region replication traffic and limiting stale reads to non-critical data slices. This improves performance and reduces synchronization overhead but requires application-level logic for data distribution.

Latency Minimization Strategies

Achieving low-latency access in geo-distributed Redis setups hinges on reducing the round-trip time (RTT) between clients and the Redis node serving their requests and optimizing replication delay.

- **Read locality:** Configuring read replicas in each geographic region enables local read access with millisecond latency. This approach demands careful replica consistency monitoring and awareness of potential staleness.

- **Write locality considerations:** While writes often must be serialized at a single primary to maintain consistency, multi-primary architectures permit distributed writes at the cost of complexity in conflict resolution. Application patterns must be calibrated accordingly.

91

- **Optimized network topology:** Utilizing dedicated private network links, high-throughput cloud interconnects, or regionally proximate availability zones minimizes communication overhead. Data centers equipped with advanced network infrastructure can reduce cross-region replication latencies.

- **Compression and batching of replication log events:** Compressing propagation streams and batching multiple commands into single network transmissions reduce bandwidth usage and effective replication delay.

Consistency Models in Geo-Distributed Contexts

Consistency guarantees directly influence operational correctness, user experience, and system design. Geo-distributed Redis aligns with several consistency models, often trading off strong consistency for performance and availability:

- **Eventual consistency:** The predominant model in asynchronous replication setups, replicas eventually converge to the primary's state. During network partitions or replication lag, clients reading from a remote replica may observe stale or conflicting views.

- **Read-after-write often consistency:** Some architectures ensure that once a write completes on the primary, reads directed to the same region or replica reflect that write immediately, but cross-region synchronization remains eventual.

- **Strong consistency through consensus protocols:** Implementations using Raft or Paxos variants coordinate transactions across regions with quorum-based commits. This provides linearizability but introduces significant write latency, often measured in tens to hundreds of milliseconds depending on the geographic distribution.

The choice among these depends heavily on application requirements. Real-time financial systems, for example, mandate strong consistency and fault tolerance, often accepting elevated latency, whereas social media or analytics workloads might prioritize availability and scale, accepting eventual consistency.

Operational Considerations and Fault Tolerance

Geo-distributed Redis necessitates enhanced monitoring, failover mechanisms, and data recovery strategies:

- **Multi-region failover:** Automated detection of regional outages and promotion of replicas to primary roles must be orchestrated carefully to avoid split-brain scenarios. Coordination layers or external consensus services are often employed.

- **Data integrity verification:** Regular checksum or hash comparisons between replicas detect inconsistencies introduced by network errors or partial replication failures.

- **Backup and disaster recovery:** Geo-replication can double as a disaster recovery mechanism, with backups stored redundantly across regions. However, replication lags and transient failures call for additional snapshot and archiving policies.

- **Configuration complexity:** Managing multiple Redis nodes with region-specific configurations, network policies, and security groups requires sophisticated automation and orchestration tooling.

Example: Deploying Redis Geo-Replication Using Redis Enterprise

Redis Enterprise provides built-in support for active-active geo-distributed deployments using CRDTs. This approach abstracts replication complexity, allowing multiple writable primaries distributed across regions. The system manages conflict-free merges and automatic reconciliation to ensure eventual consistency.

```
rladmin create db geo-distributed-db redis-bdb \
    shards 3 \
    oss_cluster_name "my-redis-cluster" \
    replication disabled \
    crdt_enabled true \
    crdt_buckets 1024 \
    enable_active_active true
```

Application clients connect to their nearest primary and perform reads and writes locally with minimal latency. Changes propagate asynchronously to other regions where CRDT merges resolve conflicts deterministically, eliminating the risks of data loss or inconsistent overwrites.

```
Client (Region A) writes key X = 100
Client (Region B) concurrently writes key X = 110

After conflict-free merge:
Key X = 210 (sum of both values in G-Counter CRDT)
```

Deploying Redis across multiple data centers or cloud regions involves complex trade-offs between latency, consistency, and operational overhead. Application requirements and tolerance for stale or conflicting data largely dictate the architectural choices, whether favoring asynchronous replication with read replicas or active-active multi-primary models leveraging CRDTs or consensus protocols. Effective geo-distributed Redis deployments require sophisticated network strategies, replication optimizations, and robust operational tooling to deliver low latency and high availability in global-scale scenarios.

4.5. Disaster Recovery Planning

Effective disaster recovery planning is a cornerstone of resilient system design, ensuring data integrity and service availability in the face of unexpected failures. This requires a comprehensive strategy that integrates robust data protection mechanisms, precise restoration procedures, and seamless failback execution to minimize downtime and data loss. The following discussion elaborates on four pivotal components: the establishment of backups, the synergistic use of Append-Only Files (AOF) and Redis Database (RDB) snapshots, meticulous restore operations planning, and the implementation of failback protocols.

Establishing Reliable Backup Strategies

Backups serve as the fundamental defense against data loss, forming the basis for any recovery effort. For mission-critical systems, a multi-tiered backup strategy is essential. Typically, this involves a combination of full and incremental backups, scheduled to balance performance overhead and recovery point objectives (RPO).

Full backups capture the entire dataset at a certain point in time but are resource-intensive. Incremental backups, which record only changes since the last backup, reduce storage and bandwidth requirements but complicate the restore process. A pragmatic approach often involves periodic full backups augmented by incremental snapshots in between.

Automated backup scheduling should be integrated with monitoring and alerting systems to promptly detect failures or missed backups. Additionally, backup storage must be geographically isolated from primary data centers to prevent concurrent loss due to site-level incidents.

Combined AOF and RDB Approaches

Redis supports two primary persistence mechanisms: RDB snapshots and Append-Only Files (AOF). Each exhibits trade-offs in durability, speed, and recovery complexity, but their combined use yields significant reliability advantages.

The RDB persistence approach generates point-in-time snapshots

95

of the dataset by serializing its state to disk. These snapshots are compact and enable fast restart times. However, since snapshots occur at scheduled intervals, data between snapshots may be lost upon failure.

Conversely, AOF captures every write operation received by the database, appending it sequentially to disk. This mechanism offers near real-time durability, as changes are typically flushed to disk multiple times per second. The downside lies in resultant file size growth and slower recovery due to replaying the entire log.

A hybrid strategy leverages the strengths of both: configuring Redis to perform periodic RDB snapshots for fast baseline restoration, supplemented by AOF logs for incremental recovery of recent changes. Redis provides configuration options to rewrite AOF files periodically, compacting them to reduce size and maintain performance. This synergy improves data safety and reduces recovery time objective (RTO).

```
save 900 1          # Save snapshot every 900 seconds if at least
    1 key changed
appendonly yes      # Enable AOF persistence
appendfsync everysec  # Fsync every second for balance of speed
    and durability
auto-aof-rewrite-percentage 100  # Trigger AOF rewrite to compact
    if file doubled in size
auto-aof-rewrite-min-size 64mb    # Ensure minimal AOF size for
    rewrites
```

This setup ensures data is captured frequently and restored efficiently while controlling resource consumption.

Planning Restore Operations

An effective disaster recovery plan mandates rigorous design and validation of restore procedures. Restoration begins with identifying the most recent consistent dataset, typically represented by the latest RDB snapshot, followed by AOF replay to recover subsequent changes.

The restore process includes the following essential steps:

1. **Locate Backup Artifacts:** Backup metadata management systems should track timestamps and storage locations of backups to swiftly identify candidates for restoration.

2. **Validate Backup Integrity:** Use checksums and digital signatures to verify backup integrity before restoration to prevent corruption propagation.

3. **Stop Service and Isolate Environment:** Halt the running database instance to prevent inconsistencies; execute restores in an isolated or sandboxed environment to safeguard ongoing operations.

4. **Restore RDB Snapshot:** Load the snapshot into Redis's data directory, ensuring permissions and ownership align with the Redis process.

5. **Replay the AOF:** Apply the append-only log file incrementally, reconstructing transactions executed after the snapshot was taken.

6. **Perform Consistency Checks:** Validate the restored dataset for application-level invariants and data coherence.

7. **Restart the Service:** Once verified, bring the Redis instance back online and monitor behavior closely during the initial period.

Automating the restore process with orchestration tools reduces manual intervention and human error, enabling rapid recovery. Recovery drills should be periodically conducted to validate the restore workflow and adjust scripts or procedures as necessary.

Implementing Seamless Failback Procedures

Failback—the process of reverting operations from a temporary recovery environment back to the primary production system—demands precision to prevent data loss, inconsistency, or downtime extension.

Fundamental considerations in failback include:

- **Data Consistency:** Confirm that all transactions performed during the failover period are synchronized with the original production environment. Typically, this requires capturing deltas in data and coordinating their reconciliation.

- **Minimal Downtime:** Design failback mechanisms to operate incrementally or asynchronously, reducing service interruption. Techniques such as dual-writing or write forwarding during failover help maintain continuity.

- **Validation and Verification:** Prior to switching operations back, run integrity tests and compare dataset hashes or checksums between failover and primary systems.

- **Rollback Capability:** Maintain the ability to revert the failback swiftly should any anomalies arise, ensuring high availability.

A common failback pattern involves leveraging replication streams. For instance, after resuming the primary Redis instance, it can be configured as a replica of the failover server to synchronize outstanding changes. Once fully synchronized, the primary is promoted to master, and clients are redirected accordingly.

```
# On primary Redis (now replica during failback)
SLAVEOF <failover_host> <failover_port>

# Monitor synchronization progress, then
SLAVEOF NO ONE   # Promote to master once caught up
```

Coordinated DNS or load balancer updates complete the failback by redirecting client traffic.

To support robust failback, recovery documentation must detail the exact sequence of commands, configuration parameter adjustments, and validation checkpoints. Continuous improvement and automation of these steps substantially increase confidence and reduce human error in crisis situations.

Cumulatively, a comprehensive disaster recovery plan that combines systematic backups, hybrid AOF/RDB persistence, well-defined restore operations, and carefully engineered failback techniques ensures data protection and service continuity. These strategies must be tailored to organizational requirements, regularly tested, and integrated into broader business continuity frameworks for optimal resilience.

4.6. Consistency and Fault Tolerance

Data consistency and fault tolerance are fundamental concerns in distributed systems, necessitating carefully designed mechanisms to ensure correctness, availability, and durability under diverse failure modes. Redis, as an in-memory data structure store, provides distinct consistency guarantees and fault tolerance behaviors that vary considerably between its standalone and clustered deployments. Understanding these behaviors requires a detailed examination of Redis's replication model, failure detection strategies, and partition handling protocols.

Redis in standalone mode employs a primary-replica replication architecture. The primary node accepts writes, which asynchronously propagate to replicas. Asynchronous replication inherently results in eventual consistency: replicas lag behind the primary, potentially leading to lost writes if the primary fails before propagating updates. While Redis supports synchronous replication via the WAIT command, which blocks the primary until a specified number of replicas acknowledge a write, this mechanism offers only limited durability guarantees, as acknowledged writes can still be lost during network partitions or node failures prior to persistence on stable storage.

During network partitions in standalone mode, consistency is impacted primarily by the absence of coordination among replicas. The single primary continues serving writes and updates replicas upon reconnection. However, if the primary fails and a replica assumes the primary role (manually or via external tools such as Redis Sentinel), there exists a risk of lost writes that had not yet propagated, manifesting as data divergence or write loss.

Redis Sentinel addresses fault tolerance by orchestrating automatic failover of primaries within a monitored replication group. Sentinel continuously monitors node health through a combination of ping-like probes and quorum-based agreement on node availability. When the primary becomes unresponsive, Sentinels collectively elect a new primary from existing replicas and update the topology, allowing writes to resume. Sentinel mitigates split-brain scenarios by requiring a majority quorum to authorize failover, minimizing the risk of multiple primaries.

In distributed environments prone to network partitions, Sentinel's approach attempts to preserve availability at the cost of potential write loss, conforming broadly to an *AP* (availability and partition-tolerance) stance in the CAP paradigm for standalone Redis deployments with Sentinel, with eventual consistency guaranteed post-recovery.

Redis Cluster extends Redis with native sharding and distributed fault tolerance, subdividing the keyspace into 16,384 hash slots distributed among cluster nodes. Each node can serve as a primary for a subset of slots, with one or more replicas. Cluster nodes communicate via a gossip protocol that disseminates membership and slot allocation information.

The cluster enforces consistency through an asynchronous replication model analogous to standalone deployments but incorporates complex failure detection and reconfiguration protocols to maintain cluster correctness under node failures and partitions. When a primary node fails, its replicas autonomously promote one to primary by consensus among the cluster nodes, avoiding manual intervention. This consensus depends on a majority vote from a subset of nodes known as *quorum*.

During network partitions, the cluster's design aims to prevent *split-brain*, a scenario where multiple primaries concurrently accept writes for the same hash slots. This is achieved by leveraging the concept of *majority quorums* for failover: a failed primary can be replaced only if a majority of its configured replicas are reachable and agree on the failover. Isolated partitions unable to form a quorum avoid failovers, rendering the affected hash slots temporarily unavailable or read-only, thereby favoring consistency over availability.

This behavior means Redis Cluster is designed to prioritize *CP* (consistency and partition tolerance) within CAP constraints, sacrificing availability for correctness during partitions. The cluster supports partial availability by marking unreachable shards as failed, while servicing reachable ones without risking data divergence. This prevents multiple primaries for the same slot but exposes clients to temporary unavailability.

Lost writes remain a risk if a primary receives a write, crashes before replication, and its designated replica fails to promote appropriately. Redis mitigates such risk by enabling the `min-slaves-to-write` and `min-slaves-max-lag` configuration options in standalone mode, and analogous parameters in Cluster mode, which restrict writes unless a minimum number of replicas acknowledge the primary's state, effectively enforcing synchronous or quasi-synchronous replication semantics under normal operations.

Furthermore, Redis Cluster uses the `CONFIG REWRITE` and `CLUSTER FAILOVER` commands to manage failovers and configuration updates that maintain cluster state correctness. Reconciliation mechanisms on node restart rely on gossip exchange and, optionally, incremental resynchronization to correct inconsistencies resulting from partitions or crashes.

Handling surviving network outages in Redis depends on the type and duration of the outage. Short outages, where nodes can reconnect and synchronize rapidly, allow the cluster to recover fully with minimal impact on correctness or availability. Extended or permanent partitions, however, may lead Redis Cluster to mark nodes as failed, evict hash slots, and limit command servicing on minority partitions to prevent stale writes.

Redis delivers a dual-faceted approach to consistency and fault tolerance: standalone deployments with Sentinel favor high availability and eventual consistency, tolerating brief inconsistencies in exchange for uninterrupted service, while Redis Cluster emphasizes consistency and partition tolerance by requiring consensus for failovers and temporarily sacrificing availability in case of network partitions. Each approach integrates failure detection, quorum-based decision-making, and replication safeguards to mitigate data loss and split-brain risks, enabling Redis to maintain correctness and operational reliability across diverse production scenarios.

Chapter 5

Performance Engineering and Monitoring

Redis consistently impresses with its speed, but sustaining peak performance at scale is an engineering challenge in its own right. In this chapter, we dissect the inner workings of Redis, revealing essential tools, diagnostics, and optimization strategies that separate ordinary deployments from truly outstanding systems. Discover how to master resource management, reveal hidden bottlenecks, and implement proactive monitoring—ensuring your Redis infrastructure never misses a beat, even in the most demanding environments.

5.1. Memory Management and Eviction Policies

Redis employs a sophisticated memory management system designed to maximize performance while respecting configured memory limits. Understanding its internal allocation strategies, fragmentation handling, and eviction algorithms is critical for tuning Redis deployments in diverse workload environments.

At the core of Redis's memory management is its use of the jemalloc allocator (or the system allocator if configured otherwise), which allocates memory in chunks optimized for small objects, minimizing overhead and fragmentation. Redis structures all data as objects with reference counting, facilitating efficient reuse and precise control of memory lifetimes. To further combat fragmentation, Redis employs periodic defragmentation routines that consolidate free space, especially when large numbers of keys are created and deleted.

Redis allows memory consumption to be capped via the `maxmemory` configuration directive. When this threshold is approached, Redis triggers eviction policies to free space without restarting or crashing. The eviction mechanism transparently deletes keys based on selected algorithms, trading off latency, data freshness, and resource usage.

The primary eviction policies supported are:

- **Least Recently Used (LRU):** Evicts keys that have been idle the longest. Redis approximates true LRU using a probabilistic sampling of keys since full LRU tracking is cost-prohibitive in large datasets. The `allkeys-lru` policy evicts from all keys, while `volatile-lru` only evicts keys with an `expire` set. LRU is ideal for caching scenarios where frequently accessed data should be kept.

- **Least Frequently Used (LFU):** Evicts keys with the low-

104

est access frequency. Redis maintains a limited precision counter to track access frequency, updated during key reads. The allkeys-lfu and volatile-lfu variants function similarly to their LRU counterparts. LFU excels in workloads with stable popularity distributions but dynamic temporal locality.

- **First In First Out (FIFO):** Evicts keys in the order they were added. This simple policy is rarely recommended unless workload semantics align with insertion order sensitivity.

- **No Eviction:** Disables eviction and returns an error on write commands when memory limit is reached, preventing unexpected data loss but requiring external monitoring for memory pressure.

Selecting the appropriate eviction policy depends crucially on workload characteristics. For typical caching use cases, allkeys-lru is a robust default, balancing recency with eviction cost. For datasets where access frequency matters more than recency, allkeys-lfu can achieve better hit rates but at the expense of more complex bookkeeping overhead. In scenarios demanding strict data retention or persistence semantics, disabling eviction and monitoring memory externally is prudent.

Redis provides tunable parameters to control the aggressiveness of eviction. The maxmemory-samples parameter adjusts the number of random keys sampled when deciding which key to evict, trading off CPU usage and eviction precision. Increasing sample size improves selection quality but incurs more CPU overhead during eviction. The lfu-log-factor and lfu-decay-time govern the LFU counter's sensitivity and decay rate, allowing fine-grained control over frequency aging.

Out-of-memory (OOM) conditions can have catastrophic effects, such as failed write operations or server crashes if not guarded properly. Redis's eviction policies serve as proactive mechanisms to maintain memory usage below maxmemory. Additionally, application-level techniques such as key expiration policies and the use of memory-efficient data structures (e.g., hashes with small integers encoded) help reduce pressure. Redis also tracks memory fragmentation and fragmentation ratios; monitoring these metrics can preclude performance degradation due to allocator inefficiencies.

Memory fragmentation is a crucial aspect of Redis's memory profile. Internally, fragmentation arises due to jemalloc's free-list management and the highly dynamic allocation patterns of small Redis objects. Redis includes a special MEMORY PURGE command that prompts jemalloc to release unused memory back to the OS, useful in long-running servers with fluctuating memory demands. Effective fragmentation management involves proper configuration of maxmemory to accommodate peak usage and regular monitoring of fragmentation reports from INFO memory.

Maximizing throughput under memory constraints involves balancing eviction policy overhead, memory fragmentation, and eviction latency. LRU and LFU policies, while effective, introduce periodic CPU overhead due to sampling and counter updates; these costs can be minimized by adjusting parameters to target workload demands. FIFO, although simpler, can cause suboptimal cache hit ratios, increasing backend load. Non-eviction configurations yield maximal data retention but require rigorous application design to avoid abrupt failure.

In distributed Redis deployments, memory management must consider replication and persistence overhead. For instance, snapshotting and append-only file rewriting temporarily increase memory usage, and eviction decisions impact data consistency across replicas. Thus, eviction policies should be coordinated with replication lag and persistence schedules.

Redis's memory management framework integrates advanced allocation techniques and multiple eviction strategies, each suitable for specific workload patterns. Proper tuning of eviction policies, sampling parameters, and memory limits enables resilient and performant Redis instances that maintain high throughput while preventing OOM scenarios. Monitoring fragmentation and memory usage metrics in conjunction with these configurations ensures sustainable operation under heavy load and evolving data sizes.

5.2. Profiling and Benchmarking Redis Systems

Effective performance measurement of Redis systems requires a blend of synthetic benchmarking tools and real-world profiling techniques to capture both theoretical limits and operational behaviors under realistic workloads. At the core of this process lies a disciplined approach to workload simulation, baseline establishment, and comprehensive analysis to uncover bottlenecks and define optimization strategies.

The most widely adopted benchmarking utility for Redis is `redis-benchmark`, a synthetic stress tool designed to simulate a variety of client operations and data patterns, providing immediate quantification of throughput and latency under configurable parameters. It enables testing for different commands (e.g., SET, GET, LPUSH, SADD) through adjustable request rates, pipeline depths, and concurrent client numbers. This flexibility allows generation of steady-state load profiles reflective of isolated Redis commands, which helps in determining peak capacity and command-specific performance envelopes.

A basic `redis-benchmark` invocation might appear as follows:

```
redis-benchmark -c 50 -n 100000 -d 1024 -t set,get -P 16
```

Here, -c 50 specifies 50 concurrent clients, -n 100000 the total requests, -d 1024 the data size per request in bytes, -t set,get the command set to benchmark, and -P 16 pipeline depth for asynchronous request dispatch. Output typically reports requests per second and average latency, allowing the establishment of baseline throughput metrics:

```
====== SET ======
  50000 requests completed in 1.23 seconds
  40 parallel clients
  16 bytes payload
  keep alive: 1

99.87% <= 2 milliseconds
1234.56 requests per second

====== GET ======
  50000 requests completed in 1.27 seconds
  40 parallel clients
  16 bytes payload
  keep alive: 1

99.95% <= 1 millisecond
1176.47 requests per second
```

While redis-benchmark excels at synthetic load generation, real-world profiling involves capturing operational metrics during production-like scenarios. This requires instrumenting the Redis server and its client environment with detailed monitoring, including latency distribution profiling, CPU utilization, memory consumption, and network I/O statistics. The Redis Slow Log feature is invaluable for pinpointing commands exceeding latency thresholds, identifying hotspots in query execution times. Profiling can be further enhanced by enabling Redis latency monitoring commands such as LATENCY LATEST, LATENCY HISTOGRAM, and LATENCY DOCTOR, which provide insights into transient latency spikes and their causal factors.

Workload simulation that mirrors production environments demands large-scale data sets and realistic request mixes. Typically, representative read/write ratios, key size distributions, and command diversity are modeled based on application trace analysis. Open-source tools such as Memtier_Benchmark extend benchmarking capabilities by supporting more flexible workload mixes, including multithreaded clients, complex command sequences, and varied keyspace designs. This allows more precise replication of application interaction patterns and uncovers performance variations attributable to workload skew or data locality effects.

Establishing a performance baseline involves running a controlled benchmark on a dedicated Redis instance with no external noise and standardized hardware conditions. System-level counters such as CPU clocks, context switches, and disk/network throughput metrics collected via tools like perf, iostat, and netstat complement Redis metrics to identify resource saturation points. Combining these observations facilitates distinguishing between intrinsic Redis limitations (e.g., command serialization, data structure overhead) and external system constraints (e.g., disk I/O bottlenecks, network saturation).

To identify true performance limits, it is critical to vary workload characteristics and environmental conditions systematically. This includes scaling the number of client connections, varying command pipeline depths, altering data persistence configurations (e.g., RDB snapshot intervals, AOF rewrite policies), and toggling clustering or replication features. Observing how throughput and latency respond to these variables reveals Redis's sensitivity to workload concurrency and durability guarantees, highlighting trade-offs between consistency, availability, and performance.

Another advanced technique involves using flame graphs to profile Redis' CPU usage and call stack behavior during high-load conditions. These graphical representations pinpoint expensive functions and inefficient code paths within the Redis server and associated libraries. Integrating flame graph analysis with latency histograms produces a rich performance profile capable of guiding code-level or configuration optimizations.

Finally, comprehensive benchmarking must incorporate failure scenarios and recovery behaviors. Testing Redis under failover, network partition, or memory pressure conditions verifies the robustness of performance under degraded modes. These stress tests entail coordinated scripts that induce faults while monitoring response times and throughput degradation, ensuring that service-level objectives remain within acceptable bounds even during anomalies.

Profiling and benchmarking Redis systems demand a methodical combination of synthetic benchmarks, realistic workload emulation, detailed metric collection, and failure scenario testing. Each step contributes to a holistic understanding of Redis performance boundaries and operational characteristics critical for tuning, capacity planning, and architecture design in high-demand environments.

5.3. Latency Analysis and Optimization

Latency in Redis operations is a critical performance metric, profoundly influencing application responsiveness and user experience. Understanding the multifaceted sources of latency is essential for precise diagnosis and effective mitigation. Redis latency arises from several stages: network transmission, command parsing and execution, background processes, and system-level constraints. Each stage contributes variably to the overall delay, necessitating targeted analysis and optimization strategies.

At the network layer, latency stems from physical distance, network congestion, and protocol overhead. The round-trip time (RTT) between client and server sets a fundamental lower bound on achievable latency. Even with ultra-low-latency processing within Redis, significant network delays can dominate the observed latency. TCP handshakes, packet retransmissions, and slow acknowledgment cycles further inflate these times. Optimizing network latency involves both infrastructure and protocol-level improvements. Strategies include colocating Redis nodes closer to clients, employing high-bandwidth, low-jitter interconnects, and leveraging technology such as RDMA (Remote Direct Memory Access) to bypass kernel networking stacks. Additionally, pipeline command batching reduces per-command RTT penalties, amortizing network latency over multiple requests.

Command handling latency within Redis itself is influenced primarily by the nature of the command, data structure complexity, and server load. Simple key retrieval commands like GET typically operate with constant time complexity $O(1)$, resulting in minimal execution latency. Conversely, commands operating on aggregated or sorted data structures, such as ZRANGE or SORT, exhibit higher latency due to traversals or temporary allocations. Latency spikes often arise when commands initiate background operations, for example, dataset persistence through the BGSAVE command or eviction triggered in maxmemory policies. These background jobs compete for CPU and I/O resources, causing transient delays observable as latency spikes.

Internally, Redis uses a single-threaded event loop to process commands sequentially, which imposes intrinsic limits on throughput and latency under high concurrency. Command execution delays can accumulate as queues lengthen, particularly if complex commands block the event loop. To assess these internal latencies, Redis provides built-in latency monitoring tools such as the LATENCY command suite. Commands like LATENCY DOCTOR and LATENCY LATEST diagnose common latency sources and report statistical distributions. Advanced profiling can be performed through the Redis slowlog, which records commands exceeding user-defined latency thresholds, facilitating identification of persistent bottlenecks.

In latency-sensitive applications, maintaining bounds on worst-case and p99 (99th percentile) latencies is paramount. Worst-case latency represents the longest execution time under any circumstance, while p99 latency characterizes the tail behavior, crucial for

Service Level Agreements (SLAs). Reducing tail latency requires a combination of architectural and operational practices:

- **Command Optimization**: Select commands and data structures with predictable, low time complexity. Avoid commands with unbounded time or memory complexity. For example, prefer HGET over iterative scans for hash retrieval.

- **Pipeline and Lua Scripting**: Group multiple commands into pipelines or atomic Lua scripts to minimize network RTTs and reduce event loop switching overhead.

- **Connection Pooling and Client-Side Sharding**: Distribute load across multiple Redis instances to prevent hotspots and overloading of single nodes, thereby lowering queue-induced latency.

- **Background Job Scheduling**: Schedule heavy tasks during off-peak hours or throttle background operations, such as AOF rewriting, to prevent contention with foreground requests.

- **Resource Provisioning**: Ensure adequate CPU and memory resources; Redis performance deteriorates markedly if server memory exceeds physical limits and swaps to disk.

For diagnosing intermittent latency spikes, external monitoring tools such as Prometheus combined with Grafana enable continuous tracking of latency metrics across clusters. Integrating Redis latency outputs into these systems provides temporal correlation with environmental factors, such as network events, garbage collection on client hosts, or operating system interrupts. Additionally, kernel-level tracing tools like perf or eBPF-based utilities can reveal blocking syscalls or CPU scheduling delays affecting Redis processes.

Adaptive techniques, including request rate limiting and backpressure, help maintain steady latency by preventing overload conditions. Load shedding mechanisms may prioritize critical queries over low-priority ones during peak loads, ensuring that p99 latency targets are met for essential operations. Another advanced technique involves tailoring Redis eviction policies to minimize locking and paging delays: for example, using `volatile-lru` instead of `allkeys-random` to reduce cache misses and induced latencies.

Measured improvements in latency often come from tuning Redis configuration parameters. For example, adjusting `hz`, which controls the frequency of Redis internal housekeeping tasks, can impact latency jitter. A high `hz` reduces latency spikes due to faster eviction and expiration processes but increases CPU usage, so trade-offs must be carefully evaluated.

Monitoring latency at granular levels using histograms or quantile summaries enables precise thresholding for triggering alerts or automated mitigation. Integrating Redis latency monitoring with deployment orchestration frameworks supports proactive scaling or configuration changes in response to detected latency degradations.

Latency in Redis operations is a composite outcome of network constraints, command characteristics, system resource contention, and background processing. A deep understanding of these sources, combined with targeted application of profiling, architectural adjustments, and operational tuning, is essential for superior latency performance. Achieving tight bounds on both worst-case and p99 latencies ensures Redis deployments fulfill demands of modern high-throughput, low-latency applications.

5.4. Hot Keys, Hot Slots, and Load Imbalance

In high-concurrency distributed systems, the distribution of incoming workload across processing units, shards, or partitions fundamentally affects overall system efficiency and fairness. A recurring and problematic phenomenon observed in such environments involves the presence of *hot keys* or *hot slots*, where a disproportionate fraction of the traffic is directed toward a small subset of the keyspace or partitions. This heavily skewed access pattern leads to *load imbalance*, causing resource saturation, increased latency, and degraded quality of service.

Keys are often hashed or otherwise mapped deterministically to logical units of storage or computation, e.g., partitions or shards, which are then allocated across nodes. Despite uniform hashing designs aiming to scatter keys evenly, real-world request patterns exhibit temporal and spatial skews. Some keys—called *hot keys*—receive disproportionately high request volumes, causing their associated processing units or *slots* to become overloaded or *hot*. Similarly, the concept of *hot slots* refers to cases where certain partitions or hash buckets themselves bear a heavier traffic burden, irrespective of the specific keys they contain.

This imbalance results in system bottlenecks: nodes responsible for hot slots exhibit high CPU use, long queue lengths, and elevated latency, while others remain underutilized. The non-uniformity of workload not only impacts throughput but also violates service-level agreements (SLAs), especially in real-time data processing or low-latency online services where predictability is critical.

Efficient detection of hot keys or hot slots is paramount for prompt corrective action. Two primary detection approaches are employed:

- **Statistical Monitoring.** Continuous collection of granular metrics such as per-key request counts, latency distributions, and queue lengths reveals skewed hot spots. Sliding-window aggregation and exponentially weighted moving averages (EWMA) help in smoothing short-term fluctuations while detecting persistent hot keys. Threshold-based triggers alert the system when certain keys or slots exceed expected request volume or latency.

- **Sketching and Approximate Counting.** For systems with massive keyspaces, maintaining exact counts is often infeasible. Techniques like Count-Min Sketch or Heavy Hitters algorithms efficiently approximate the frequency of keys, enabling identification of the most frequent keys (heavy hitters) whose cumulative load surpasses predefined thresholds. These algorithms operate in sublinear space and support incremental updates in streaming fashion, making them well-suited for high-throughput environments.

Detection must balance fidelity and overhead: overly frequent or fine-grained monitoring can degrade performance, while coarse or delayed detection risks prolonged imbalance.

Load imbalance stemming from hot keys or slots manifests in multiple system symptoms:

- *Increased Tail Latency:* Hot shards develop long request queues, causing increased variance and longer tail latencies, undermining user experience or downstream pipeline stability.

- *Reduced Throughput:* Overburdened partitions become bottlenecks, limiting maximum request processing rates despite available capacity elsewhere.

- *Resource Contention:* Hot nodes experience contention in CPU, memory, and I/O, increasing the risk of thrashing, failures, or fallback to throttling policies, which degrade overall robustness.

Understanding these consequences underlines the need for effective and adaptive load rebalancing strategies.

To counteract hot keys and hot slots, systems incorporate *dynamic rebalancing* mechanisms that redistribute load and restore fairness. These remedial techniques can be broadly categorized as follows:

Key Splitting and Fine-Grained Partitioning. Reconceptualizing partitions at a finer granularity enables more flexible migration of load. Systems may split a hot key's traffic across multiple sub-keys or shards by suffixing keys with extra bits or hashing the original keys into secondary partitions. This approach reduces per-shard skew while maintaining logical consistency through aggregation layers.

Adaptive Hashing and Consistent Rehashing. Instead of static hashing, adaptive schemes dynamically reassign keys or slots to different nodes based on current load metrics. Consistent hashing variants with virtual nodes allow hot partitions to be split by introducing additional virtual nodes that map portions of the hot slot to less loaded physical nodes. This avoids large-scale data reshuffling and amortizes migration costs.

Weighted Load Distribution. Nodes and partitions can be assigned weights proportional to their processing capacity or network bandwidth. The hashing schemes factor in these weights, directing traffic preferentially so that overloaded nodes receive a smaller proportion of keys, mitigating imbalance.

Work Stealing and Request Redirection. At runtime, overloaded nodes may offload excess requests to underutilized peers via coordinated work-stealing, request forwarding, or proxying layers. Although this incurs additional network overhead and complexity, it provides a transient mechanism to absorb spikes in load without immediate redistribution.

Rate Limiting and Backpressure. As a complement to load

redistribution, systems often implement rate limiting on hot keys or clients generating hot traffic to protect overall system health. While rate limiting directly reduces imbalance by throttling, it must be carefully balanced to avoid unfair penalization or cascading degradation.

Designing effective dynamic rebalancing entails addressing several challenges:

- **Latency Sensitivity:** Rebalancing operations that migrate state or partition ownership should minimize disruption and data movement to avoid service degradation. Techniques such as incremental migration, dual ownership, or temporary replication facilitate smooth transitions.

- **Consistency and Ordering.** For stateful services, splitting or migration must preserve consistency guarantees and operation ordering, often requiring transactional metadata or careful synchronization protocols.

- **Detection Responsiveness vs. Stability.** Aggressive rebalancing triggered by transient spikes can induce oscillations and thrashing. Incorporation of hysteresis, smoothing, and cooldown intervals helps stabilize behavior.

- **Monitoring Overheads.** High-resolution telemetry and frequent load reporting generate overhead; sampling, aggregation, and approximation methods help maintain monitoring scalability.

- **Heterogeneous Environments.** Nodes may vary in capacity, network topology, or locality constraints. Load balancing policies must respect these constraints to avoid suboptimal placement.

Consider a distributed key-value store partitioned using consistent hashing. Despite uniform hashing, access patterns frequently produce hot keys, such as popular session IDs or trending items.

Detection relies on a Count-Min Sketch maintained on each node to approximate per-key request counts over 1-minute windows, aggregated centrally to identify heavy hitters. Upon detection, the system splits the hot keys into multiple virtual sub-keys, each mapped to different virtual nodes, and migrates corresponding data subsets to underutilized nodes. A coordination protocol ensures clients receive updated routing metadata.

The result is a marked reduction in tail latency for operations on hot keys, along with more balanced CPU utilization across nodes. Further, backpressure mechanisms selectively limit bursty clients to avoid immediate overload while migration completes.

This systematic approach exemplifies the synergy between detection algorithms, dynamic partitioning, and coordinated migration in taming hot keys and maintaining system equilibrium.

Understanding and mitigating the effects of hot keys and hot slots remain pivotal to achieving high throughput and predictable latency in modern concurrent systems. By leveraging scalable detection, adaptive partitioning, and coordination protocols, distributed architectures can maintain service fairness and resilience in the face of unpredictable traffic patterns.

5.5. Operational Metrics and Instrumentation

Effective monitoring of Redis instances hinges upon the strategic collection and interpretation of key operational metrics. These metrics offer visibility into Redis performance, health, and utilization patterns and are indispensable for maintaining high availability, diagnosing issues, and optimizing workloads. This section focuses on the most critical Redis metrics, their intrinsic significance, and pragmatic guidelines for collection and alerting. The discussed tools include commandstats, the slowlog, keyspace notifications, along with consolidated operational insights derived from these sources.

Command Statistics (commandstats)

The commandstats section in the Redis INFO command output provides granular statistics on each Redis command executed since server startup. It reports invocation counts, cumulative execution times, and average latencies per command. Monitoring these data points enables precise profiling of command workload distribution and latency characteristics.

- **Invocation Counts**: A sudden spike in the frequency of specific commands may suggest changes in application behavior or potential abuse.

- **Average Latency**: Calculated as total microseconds spent on a command divided by its calls, this metric highlights commands that contribute disproportionately to server load.

- **Total Time Spent**: Commands consuming excessive CPU or I/O resources over time warrant investigation or optimization.

Commands with inherently higher complexity, such as SORT, ZRANGE, or EVAL, should be closely monitored for latency growth, as unexpected increases often indicate growing data set sizes or suboptimal query patterns. Best practices involve collecting commandstats metrics at frequent intervals (e.g., every 30 seconds to 1 minute), storing historical trends, and setting alert thresholds on both the absolute latency and relative changes in command execution patterns.

Slow Log (slowlog)

The Redis slowlog captures commands whose execution duration exceeds a configurable threshold (default 10 ms), retaining detailed entries including the command, execution time in microseconds, and timestamps.

- **Significance**: The slowlog serves as a critical diagnostic tool for identifying performance bottlenecks caused by expensive commands executed either sporadically or as part of high-frequency workloads.

- **Configuration**: Adjust the `slowlog-log-slower-than` parameter to tune sensitivity according to system performance baselines.

- **Operational Use**: Periodic analysis of slowlog entries reveals inefficiencies such as scanning large sorted sets or inefficient Lua scripts.

Integrating slowlog inspections into automated alerts is highly recommended. For instance, alerting on slowlog length growth or the reappearance of specific slow commands facilitates proactive intervention before user experience degradation.

Keyspace Notifications

Redis supports `keyspace notifications`, which emit events on key modifications, expirations, evictions, and other changes. These notifications can be enabled selectively through the `notify-keyspace-events` configuration parameter.

- **Utility**: Keyspace notifications aid in operational visibility by signaling real-time changes in cache or data state without continuous polling.

- **Use Cases**: They can trigger asynchronous workflows, update derived state, or serve as early warnings for key eviction or expiration trends.

- **Best Practices**: Enable only necessary event classes to minimize overhead, for example, focusing on expiration events Ex or eviction events Ev. Employ dedicated Pub/Sub listeners to consume these events reliably.

Capturing keyspace events enables behavioral pattern recognition such as cache churn or anomaly detection in access patterns, thereby providing actionable operational insights.

Synthesizing Metrics for Operational Insights

Real-time operational decision-making benefits from synthesizing the above metrics:

- Correlating command latency spikes (from `commandstats`) with slowlog entries helps pinpoint causative commands and their impact.

- Identifying patterns in keyspace notifications can illuminate rapid key expiry or eviction rates, signaling potential memory pressure or misconfigured TTL policies.

- Tracking frequent transitions in command execution counts may reveal application-side issues like retry storms or unexpected workload shifts.

Collection and Alerting Best Practices

- **Metric Collection**: Use automated monitoring agents or custom scripts to query `INFO` commandstats and slowlog regularly. Maintain time-series storage for trend analysis.

- **Aggregation**: Summarize data over sliding windows (e.g., 5 minutes) to smooth transient fluctuations and better detect sustained anomalies.

- **Alerting Strategies**: Establish multi-threshold alerts—for example, a warning threshold on average latency increase with a critical alert on exceeding absolute latency limits or on slowlog count growth.

- **Capacity Planning**: Use historical metric trends to forecast resource needs, memory usage, and identify workload changes proactively.

Incorporating continuous metric collection and intelligent alerting, augmented with real-time event-driven notification processing, forms the backbone of reliable Redis operation in production environments. The interplay of these operational metrics enables rapid pinpointing and resolution of performance degradations, fostering system stability and responsiveness.

5.6. Advanced Logging and Tracing

Effective logging and tracing are indispensable for managing and debugging complex workloads, particularly in multi-layered or distributed systems. Configuring targeted logging enables developers and system administrators to collect precise diagnostic information while minimizing performance overhead and noise. Tracing, on the other hand, facilitates an end-to-end view into the system's behavior, empowering identification of bottlenecks, slow commands, and causal relationships across components.

Targeted logging requires careful selection of log levels, loggers, and filters to isolate relevant events without overwhelming downstream log processing systems. Typical log levels range from DEBUG and INFO for routine operations, to WARN and ERROR for signaling anomalous conditions. Advanced configurations employ dynamic log level adjustments, either programmatically or via centralized management, to raise verbosity only for components involved in a suspected issue. For example, a high-frequency cache subsystem may normally log only warnings, but during investigations, enabling detailed debug logs selectively reveals timing and state transitions.

Tracing enhances visibility beyond static log messages by capturing the causal flow of requests and operations through a system. Distributed tracing, in particular, attaches unique trace identifiers to requests as they traverse services, enabling the reconstruction of execution paths and analysis of latencies. Frameworks such as

OpenTelemetry provide standards for collecting, propagating, and exporting trace data in heterogeneous environments. Propagation mechanisms must be integrated within communication protocols or frameworks to pass trace context transparently through RPC calls, message queues, or asynchronous handlers.

Identifying slow commands or operations through logging and tracing involves several techniques. Instrumentation points placed strategically within critical code paths log timestamps and contextual metadata, allowing for calculation of execution durations. Metrics can be correlated with these logs to detect outliers and anomalies. For example, augmenting query execution paths with timing logs and trace spans yields visibility into slow database queries or remote API calls affecting overall performance. Alerts can be configured based on thresholds derived from these measurements to flag excessive latencies in real time.

Root cause analysis is a systematic process facilitated by well-structured logs and comprehensive traces. The diagnosis begins by identifying the symptom—a slow response, error code, or resource contention—from logs filtered by time window or severity. Tracing then reconstructs the sequence of component interactions leading to this symptom. Correlating trace identifiers with log entries enables pinpointing which microservice or subsystem experienced delays or exceptions. Additionally, extractable attributes such as error codes, configuration parameters, and environment details assist in isolating defects or misconfigurations.

Maintaining traceability in multi-layered or distributed architectures necessitates consistent application of contextual identifiers across components. This includes propagating a unique *trace ID* and a *span ID* for each segment of execution. Parent-child relationships between spans represent nested operations, preserving the causal chain. Key enrichments include tagging spans with metadata such as service version, host information, and operation type, which enhance filtering and analysis capabilities during post-mortem investigations. It is critical to implement these mechanisms uniformly across languages and platforms used by different services to ensure comprehensive observability.

Several practical considerations influence the design of an advanced logging and tracing solution:

- **Performance overhead:** Excessive logging or fine-grained tracing can introduce latency and resource consumption. Sampling strategies selectively record a subset of requests for tracing while maintaining logs at optimal levels.

- **Data storage and retention:** Large volumes of logs and trace data require scalable storage solutions and efficient query capabilities. Log aggregation frameworks and trace backends such as Elasticsearch, Jaeger, or Zipkin help organize and analyze data.

- **Security and privacy:** Logs and traces may contain sensitive information. Redaction, encryption, and access controls are necessary to comply with privacy policies and regulatory requirements.

- **Automation and integration:** Automated tooling that links alerts, dashboards, and incident management systems accelerates response to detected anomalies. APIs enabling programmatic adjustment of logging and tracing parameters support adaptive observability.

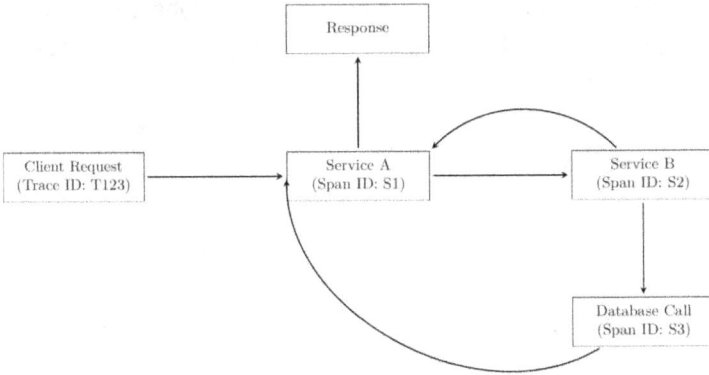

The diagram illustrates a trace propagation where a client request initiates a trace with ID T123. The trace consists of nested spans corresponding to calls across services and database operations. Each span captures timing and contextual metadata, enabling detailed performance profiling and dependency mapping.

An example of logging for a slow command within a service might be:

```
if (commandExecutionTime > SLOW_COMMAND_THRESHOLD) {
    logger.warn("Slow command detected: commandId={}, duration={}
    ms, user={}",
                commandId, commandExecutionTime, userId);
}
```

Accompanying this, the tracing system creates a span with explicit timing annotations:

```
with tracer.start_span('DatabaseQuery', child_of=parent_span) as
    span:
    span.set_attribute('db.statement', query)
    start_time = time.time()
    result = execute_query(query)
    duration = time.time() - start_time
    span.set_attribute('duration_ms', duration * 1000)
    if duration > SLOW_QUERY_THRESHOLD:
        span.set_status(Status(StatusCode.ERROR, "Slow query
        detected"))
```

Captured traces and logs combine to provide a coherent picture explaining delays. By following these methods, teams gain the ability to track performance degradation, efficiently localize faults, and maintain observability in highly complex environments with minimal disruption or overhead.

Chapter 6

Security, Access Control, and Compliance

In a world of escalating threats and stringent regulations, safeguarding your data infrastructure is not just best practice—it's imperative. This chapter uncovers how Redis can be locked down and operated securely, offering robust access controls, encrypted communication, and auditing capabilities. Go beyond default setups as you learn to design resilient Redis deployments that stand up to attackers and meet modern compliance requirements head-on.

6.1. Authentication and Role-Based Access Control

Redis incorporates sophisticated authentication and authorization capabilities designed to protect data integrity and confidentiality while supporting flexible access policies suitable for enterprise environments. Central to this security model are Access Control Lists (ACLs), which enable administrators to define granular permissions on a per-user basis. Particularly in demanding settings with multiple users and services interacting with Redis, an effective role-based access control (RBAC) strategy can enforce the principle of least privilege, minimizing attack surfaces and operational risk.

At its core, Redis authentication requires clients to supply valid credentials before issuing commands. This process begins by configuring one or more user accounts, each associated with specific passwords and command access rights. By default, Redis uses a single global password; however, the introduction of ACLs in Redis 6.0 enhanced this approach by allowing multiple users, each with independent permissions and authentication mechanisms.

The design of Redis ACLs revolves around several components:

- **Users**: Defined entities representing connections to the Redis server. Each user is assigned a username, one or more hashed passwords, and a set of command and key restrictions.

- **Command Permissions**: Fine-grained control over which commands a user can execute. This filtering helps prevent unauthorized operations, such as data deletion or configuration changes.

- **Key Patterns**: Restrictions on the keyspace a user may access, enabling segmentation of data responsibilities among roles.

The creation and management of users generally begin with the `ACL SETUSER` command, which specifies passwords and permissions in a single directive. Passwords must be stored as hashes using the SHA-256 algorithm, configured internally by Redis, ensuring that plaintext secrets are never retained on disk.

To illustrate, consider establishing a user with read-only access:

```
ACL SETUSER readonly_user on >mYp@ssw0rd ~* +@read
```

This command performs the following actions:

- Enables the user account (on flag).

- Sets the password to `mYp@ssw0rd` (hashed internally).

- Grants access to all keys via `~*`.

- Permits execution of all commands categorized under the `@read` command group.

Command categories provide an intuitive way to bundle related commands. Common categories include `@read`, `@write`, `@admin`, and `@fast`. These groupings streamline ACL definitions by abstracting command sets that share logical purposes.

Designing role-based access control with Redis ACLs involves carefully mapping organizational roles to appropriate permissions:

- **Define Roles**: Identify distinct roles such as *Reader*, *Writer*, *Administrator*, and *ServiceAccount*, each reflecting typical access patterns.

- **Assign Commands**: Allocate command groups to these roles consistent with operational needs. For example, *Reader* roles should only execute commands mapped to the `@read` category, preventing data mutation.

- **Restrict Key Access**: Limit each role to relevant keyspaces. For instance, a billing service may access keys prefixed with `billing:`, enforced with the `~` modifier.

- **Implement Password Policies**: Enforce strong password requirements, rotation schedules, and multi-password support to mitigate credential compromise.

An example for a write-enabled user restricted to specific key patterns that include sensitive metadata might be:

```
ACL SETUSER writer-user on >WriterP@ss ~billing:* +@write +@read
```

This setup grants the user rights to both write and read commands but confines access to keys with the billing: prefix only, enforcing strict compartmentalization.

Secure password management within Redis is critical. Passwords should always be set via hashed values and never transmitted or stored in cleartext. Clients authenticate using the AUTH command with the appropriate username and password:

```
AUTH writer-user WriterP@ss
```

If authentication succeeds, the server allows the client to issue commands according to the ACL restrictions. Any attempt to execute disallowed commands results in errors, thus ensuring policy enforcement.

For operational robustness, ACLs can be exported and imported via the ACL SAVE and ACL LOAD commands, enabling replication of role configurations across environments and facilitating backup strategies.

The principle of least privilege, foundational to RBAC, prescribes that each user or service is granted no more access than is necessary to perform its function. In Redis, this is effectively operationalized by:

- Minimizing the command categories assigned to users.

- Restricting keyspace access through precise pattern matching.

- Regularly reviewing and updating ACLs to reflect evolving security requirements.

Enforcing least privilege mitigates risks arising from misconfigurations or compromise of credentials, limiting potential damage.

Redis's ACL framework also supports ephemeral passwords and temporary users, which can be dynamically enabled or disabled through administrative commands, facilitating scenarios such as just-in-time access or emergency escalation, further aligning with modern security paradigms.

Redis's robust authentication mechanisms and ACL-based RBAC support enable highly secure deployment in complex, multi-user environments. Through detailed configuration of users, command permissions, key access, and secure credential management, Redis supports a rigorous authorization model that upholds best practices in modern system design.

6.2. Encryption in Transit and at Rest

Securing Redis data throughout its lifecycle necessitates robust encryption mechanisms both for data in transit and at rest. Ensuring confidentiality, authenticity, and integrity requires a multi-layered approach combining TLS/SSL encryption for network traffic, client-side encryption for sensitive payloads, and encrypted storage for persistent data. This section delineates practical strategies to implement and manage these protections, with particular emphasis on Redis configurations, certificate handling, and integration with external vaults or key management systems (KMS).

TLS/SSL for Encrypting Redis Traffic

Redis, by default, communicates in plaintext TCP, making it vulnerable to interception or tampering in untrusted networks. Enabling TLS/SSL for Redis traffic provides transport-layer confidentiality and integrity, protecting data exchanged between Redis clients and servers.

Since Redis 6, native TLS support is included, enabling encrypted connections without external proxies. To configure TLS for Redis, the server requires a private key, an appropriate X.509 certificate, and the CA certificates used to validate client certificates if mutual authentication is desired. The key configuration parameters in redis.conf are:

```
tls-port 6379
port 0
tls-cert-file /etc/redis/redis.crt
tls-key-file /etc/redis/redis.key
tls-ca-cert-file /etc/redis/ca.crt
tls-auth-clients no
```

Setting tls-port enables TLS support on the given port while disabling the unsecured port. The tls-cert-file and tls-key-file specify the Redis server's certificate and private key respectively. The tls-ca-cert-file is used for client certificate validation if client authentication is enabled by setting tls-auth-clients to yes.

To generate self-signed certificates for testing, the following OpenSSL commands suffice:

```
openssl req -newkey rsa:4096 -nodes -keyout redis.key -x509 -days
    365 -out redis.crt
openssl req -newkey rsa:4096 -nodes -keyout ca.key -x509 -days
    365 -out ca.crt
```

For production, certificate management should employ a proper Public Key Infrastructure (PKI), preferably integrated with an internal or trusted external Certificate Authority.

Redis clients must be configured to connect over TLS, specifying the CA certificate for server validation and potentially providing client certificates. For example, the redis-cli command for a TLS connection is:

```
redis-cli -h redis.example.com -p 6379 --tls --cert client.crt --
    key client.key --cacert ca.crt
```

Implementing TLS at the transport layer safeguards Redis traffic against network-level adversaries, but does not protect data stored inside Redis itself from compromise of the Redis process or storage media.

Client-Side Encryption for End-to-End Protection

Client-side encryption extends protection by encrypting sensitive data before transmission to Redis. This ensures that even if the Redis server or disk storage is compromised, plaintext data remains inaccessible without client-held keys.

Applications must integrate cryptographic libraries to encrypt data prior to sending it to Redis and decrypt upon retrieval. Common symmetric encryption schemes include AES in Galois/Counter Mode (AES-GCM) for authenticated encryption, ensuring confidentiality and integrity of data blobs.

A typical workflow:

1. Generate a strong symmetric key cached in application memory or fetched securely from a key vault.

2. Encrypt application data using AES-GCM with a random nonce before storing it in Redis.

3. Store the encrypted ciphertext (along with the nonce and any authentication tag) as the Redis value.

4. Upon retrieval, decrypt and authenticate data using the same symmetric key and nonce.

Security considerations include nonce management to prevent reuse, secure key storage on the client side, and management of encryption parameters to facilitate updates and key rotation.

Pseudocode demonstrating this operation is as follows:

```
from cryptography.hazmat.primitives.ciphers.aead import AESGCM
import os

key = b'\x00' * 32  # 256-bit key retrieved securely
aesgcm = AESGCM(key)
```

```
nonce = os.urandom(12)
plaintext = b"sensitive data"
ciphertext = aesgcm.encrypt(nonce, plaintext, associated_data=
    None)

redis.set("key", nonce + ciphertext)

# Retrieval
data = redis.get("key")
nonce_received, ciphertext_received = data[:12], data[12:]
plaintext_recovered = aesgcm.decrypt(nonce_received,
    ciphertext_received, associated_data=None)
```

Integrating client-side encryption enhances security posture by isolating encryption responsibility from Redis itself, but requires secure key management and application architecture changes.

Encrypted Storage and Integration with Key Management Systems

Redis persistence mechanisms-RDB snapshots and AOF logs-write data to disk in plaintext by default, exposing data to local compromise scenarios. Encrypting these files protects data at rest.

Since native encrypted storage is not offered by Redis, this is achieved via:

- Filesystem-level encryption, such as Linux's dm-crypt/LUKS or platform-specific encrypted volumes.

- Utilizing cloud provider storage encryption integrated transparently.

- Employing encryption plugins or modifying Redis persistence pipeline to encrypt dumps prior to writing and decrypt upon loading.

Advanced deployments integrate Redis with external Vault solutions to manage encryption keys and secrets over their life cycle. HashiCorp Vault or cloud KMS services can provide:

- Centralized key management with access policies.

- Automatic key rotation and revocation.

- Encryption-as-a-Service APIs.

- Secure injection of keys into running Redis instances or client applications at startup via environment variables or secure agents.

A typical integration scenario involves the following lifecycle:

1. Redis or client applications authenticate securely to the vault (e.g., via TLS mutual authentication or cloud identity).

2. Retrieve or request encryption keys dynamically at runtime.

3. Use vault-managed envelope encryption: data keys are used for bulk encryption, encrypted with master keys maintained by the vault.

4. Regularly rotate keys, ensuring backward compatibility by retaining prior keys for decrypting legacy data.

Configuration of these interactions depends heavily on organizational infrastructure but follows strict security principles to minimize exposure:

- Vault credentials and tokens must be ephemeral and tightly scoped.

- Keys should never be stored in code repositories or persistent configuration files.

- Audit logging at the vault level is essential for monitoring key access.

Redis modules or sidecar processes can be developed to handle encryption and decryption transparently using vault APIs, thus abstracting cryptographic complexity from application code.

Certificate Revocation and Rotation Practices

Managing certificate life cycles in TLS deployments is crucial. Redis deployments should incorporate automated certificate renewal and revocation checking mechanisms, such as:

- Utilizing Online Certificate Status Protocol (OCSP) stapling where supported.

- Automating certificate issuance and renewal with ACME protocols (e.g., Let's Encrypt with certbot) for ephemeral or public-facing environments.

- Scheduling regular rotation of private keys and certificates to reduce attack windows.

- Coordinating client and server updates to avoid service disruptions during rotations.

Combining these capabilities with robust monitoring and alert systems completes a comprehensive encryption strategy for Redis environments.

This multi-faceted approach-comprising TLS for secure transit, client-side encryption for end-to-end confidentiality, encrypted persistent storage, and integration with external vault-based key management-provides a resilient framework to safeguard Redis data across its complete life cycle. Each layer addresses distinct threat vectors and operational requirements, delivering defense in depth for mission-critical data caches.

6.3. Network Isolation and Firewalls

When deploying Redis in production environments, establishing robust network isolation and firewall policies is paramount to safeguarding the system from unauthorized access. Given Redis's default trust model, which assumes a secure network perimeter, improper network exposure poses critical security risks. Implementing best practices in firewall configuration, subnet isolation, and access restriction ensures that Redis instances remain protected against both external and internal threats.

A fundamental best practice is to avoid exposing Redis directly to public networks. Redis instances should never listen on publicly routable IP addresses unless additional layers of security such as advanced authentication and encrypted transport are rigorously employed. Instead, Redis servers should be confined to private subnets within a trusted network segment. This guarantees that only application servers or management hosts within the same subnet, or connected securely through virtual private networks (VPNs), can access Redis.

Subnet isolation is typically realized by leveraging network design principles that restrict Redis traffic to dedicated, segmented logical networks. For example, deploying Redis inside isolated Virtual Private Clouds (VPCs) or Virtual Networks (VNets) allows administrators to apply fine-grained network security policies. Within these isolated subnets, one can define routing tables, network access control lists (ACLs), and firewall rules that prevent any traffic from entering or leaving except explicitly allowed connections. This approach minimizes the attack surface by isolating Redis instances from unrelated systems and prevents lateral movement in the event of a compromise elsewhere in the network.

Firewall rules must be implemented to restrict inbound connections to only those IP addresses and ports necessary for the application to function. At a minimum, the Redis port (default 6379) should only be accessible from trusted hosts or subnet ranges. Defining explicit source IP address ranges in the firewall policy provides a strong layer of access control beyond Redis's own authentication mechanisms. Considerations for outbound traffic should also be applied; for example, preventing Redis from initiating outbound connections unless explicitly required reduces the risk of data exfiltration or command injection attacks.

In environments with multi-tenant architectures or where Redis is accessed by diverse application components, it is advisable to combine host-level firewalls (e.g., iptables or Windows Firewall) with perimeter network firewalls. Host-based firewalls provide a last line of defense and can be configured to only allow Redis client connections from known internal IPs or loopback interfaces. This dual-layer protection reduces the risk of accidental or malicious exposure caused by misconfigured external firewalls.

To further minimize exposure, Redis instances can be configured to bind exclusively to the localhost interface or internal subnet IP addresses using the bind directive in the Redis configuration file. Setting bind 127.0.0.1 restricts Redis access to local clients only, which is appropriate for scenarios where Redis runs on the same host as the client. Alternatively, specifying internal subnet IP addresses tightens control over which network interfaces Redis is accessible on. This method is complementary to firewall restrictions and acts as a safeguard if firewall rules are misapplied.

Layered security measures also include disabling Redis commands that may be exploited for reconnaissance or privilege escalation. Commands such as CONFIG, DEBUG, or FLUSHALL should be disabled or renamed when possible, limiting the potential impact of unauthorized access. These configurations, while not strictly network isolation mechanisms, reduce the internal attack surface when combined with strong firewall policies.

Zero-trust network principles can be applied to Redis deployments by enforcing mutual authentication and encryption via TLS. Enabling TLS terminates the reliance on network isolation as the sole protective model and encrypts Redis traffic, which is especially vital when crossing untrusted network boundaries or when Redis must be accessed remotely.

Monitoring and auditing network access attempts serve as complementary controls. Network intrusion detection systems (NIDS) combined with logging of firewall events can quickly highlight unusual connection patterns or unauthorized access attempts targeting Redis. Timely detection allows for rapid response, reducing the window of exposure.

The following concrete best practices are recommended for secure Redis network deployment:

- Confine Redis instances to private, isolated subnets or VLANs within the enterprise network.

- Avoid exposing Redis directly to public internet or untrusted networks.

- Use firewall rules to restrict inbound access to the Redis port(s) only from authorized IP addresses or subnets.

- Employ host-level firewalls in addition to perimeter firewalls for defense in depth.

- Configure Redis to bind only to local or internal IP interfaces using the bind directive.

- Disable or rename high-risk administrative Redis commands to reduce attack surface.

- Enable TLS encryption and strong authentication to protect traffic crossing trust boundaries.

- Continuously monitor firewall logs and network traffic for anomalous access patterns.

Implementing these layered defenses ensures that Redis instances are insulated from both external adversaries and potentially compromised internal hosts. Network isolation combined with strict firewall policies acts as a critical barrier, enabling Redis to function in highly secure and resilient production environments.

6.4. Vulnerability Management and Hardening

Effective vulnerability management and system hardening form the cornerstone of securing Redis in production environments. Given Redis's critical role in many architectures as a high-performance, in-memory data structure store, it is imperative to employ proactive measures that minimize exposure to exploits and ensure rapid recovery from incidents. The defense-in-depth model applied to Redis encompasses continuous vulnerability monitoring, prompt application of security patches, configuring Redis with robust security parameters, and establishing tailored incident response protocols.

Continuous Vulnerability Monitoring

Redis's security landscape is dynamic, evolving with the discovery of new exploits and the release of both official updates and third-party patches. Organizations must maintain continuous surveillance of Redis-related vulnerabilities. Key sources include the National Vulnerability Database (NVD), Redis official GitHub repository release notes, and security advisories from major cloud providers and third-party Redis hosting platforms.

Automated vulnerability scanners integrated into CI/CD pipelines are instrumental in identifying out-of-date Redis versions or misconfigurations. These tools can parse Redis configurations, flag risky settings (such as exposed commands or default ports), and alert administrators when a Redis instance is out of sync with the latest security standards.

Timely Patching and Upgrades

Once a security vulnerability is identified, expeditious application of patches or upgrades is critical to mitigating risk. Redis releases frequent minor updates to address security flaws, improve access controls, or fix memory corruption bugs that could lead to denial-of-service (DoS) or remote code execution. Delaying these updates increases the attack surface and the likelihood of exploitation.

Administrators should adopt a controlled upgrade strategy that balances availability with security. For clusters, this may involve incrementally upgrading nodes, verifying replication and failover behavior post-update. Using tools such as Redis Sentinel or Redis Cluster with automated failover capabilities ensures minimal downtime during patching cycles.

Backups taken prior to system updates guarantee rapid rollback if unexpected issues arise. Regular security testing post-patch deployment confirms that introduced fixes do not affect normal operation or yet leave residual vulnerabilities.

Security-Centric Configuration Options

Securing Redis begins with its configuration. By default, Redis prioritizes performance and simplicity, often leaving it vulnerable to unauthorized access if deployed without restrictions. Effective hardening includes embedding multiple protective layers through configuration directives:

- **Binding Interfaces**: By default, Redis listens on all interfaces (0.0.0.0). Restrict binding via bind directive to trusted internal IPs only to prevent external network exposure.

- **Authentication**: Enabling requirepass sets a global password mandatory for client connections. While coarse-grained, it adds a critical authentication barrier.

- **Command Renaming and Disabling**: Redis allows re-naming or disabling dangerous commands that can nega-tively impact security, such as FLUSHALL, CONFIG, and DEBUG, using the rename-command option.

- **Access Control Lists (ACLs)**: Introduced in Redis 6, ACLs provide fine-grained permission control per user, allowing explicit rights to specific commands and keyspaces. Leveraging ACLs drastically reduces privilege escalation risks within Redis.

- **Transport Layer Security (TLS)**: Redis supports TLS en-cryption to secure data in transit, preventing man-in-the-middle attacks. Configuring Redis with proper certificates, cipher suites, and client verification strengthens confiden-tiality and integrity.

- **Protected Mode**: When enabled, Redis refuses external connections by default unless explicitly configured other-wise, thereby reducing unauthorized external access.

Sample hardened configuration snippet:

```
bind 127.0.0.1 192.168.1.100
requirepass s3cureP@ssw0rd
rename-command CONFIG ""
rename-command FLUSHALL ""
aclfile /etc/redis/users.acl
tls-port 6379
tls-cert-file /etc/redis/redis.crt
tls-key-file /etc/redis/redis.key
tls-ca-cert-file /etc/redis/ca.crt
protected-mode yes
```

Defense-in-Depth Strategies

Redis security benefits from adopting multiple overlapping layers of defense, ensuring that if one control is bypassed, others limit the impact:

- **Network Segmentation**: Deploy Redis instances in iso-lated network segments, accessible only by trusted application servers and administrators, ideally behind firewalls or virtual private network (VPN) gateways.

- **Role-Based Access Controls**: Enforce strict access controls on the operating system and orchestration level where Redis runs, limiting SSH and Redis privilege escalations.

- **Audit Logging**: Enable and centralize logging of Redis access patterns, command executions, and error events. This facilitates anomaly detection and forensic investigations.

- **Rate Limiting and Connection Controls**: Limit client connection rates per IP to mitigate brute-force password guessing or denial-of-service attempts.

- **Automated Backups and Integrity Checks**: Schedule frequent backups with cryptographic verification to prevent data loss or tampering.

Together, these layers minimize attack vectors, slow adversaries, and maximize detection capabilities.

Incident Response Planning for Redis

Even with comprehensive defenses, incidents may still occur. A well-defined incident response (IR) plan tailored to Redis's operational context ensures rapid containment and recovery. Key components include:

- **Preparation**: Establish a Redis-specific IR team with clearly assigned roles and communication protocols. Pre-deploy forensic tools capable of snapshotting Redis process memory, configurations, and logs.

- **Detection and Analysis**: Monitor Redis telemetry and logs continuously with SIEM integration. Use threshold-based alerts for unusual commands, failed authentications, or connection anomalies.

- **Containment**: Upon compromise, isolate affected Redis instances from the network to prevent lateral movement. If feasible, revoke or rotate authentication credentials and keys.

- **Eradication and Recovery**: Replace compromised binaries with verified versions, reload configuration with hardened settings, and restore data from untampered backups. Validate data consistency and system integrity before resuming operations.

- **Post-Incident Review**: Conduct root cause analysis to identify exploited vulnerabilities and process gaps. Update patch management and hardening practices accordingly.

Integrating Redis into broader organizational IR workflows ensures coordinated response and minimizes impact.

The intersection of vigilant vulnerability monitoring, rigorous patch management, secure configuration, layered defenses, and a tailored incident response framework forms the foundation for resilient Redis deployments. Proactive management of Redis security properties significantly reduces the risk of compromise in environments where Redis underpins critical data operations.

6.5. Auditing and Compliance Reporting

Ensuring robust auditing and compliance reporting is fundamental for modern data stores, particularly those integrated into critical infrastructures subject to stringent regulatory frameworks. Redis, as an in-memory data structure store, offers several mechanisms and techniques to track access, log sensitive operations, and generate compliance-ready reports that can be tailored to meet diverse organizational and regulatory requirements. This section explores these techniques with emphasis on tuning Redis's auditing capabilities for regulatory adherence and effective governance.

Redis inherently provides command-level logging and access control features through its Authentication and Authorization mechanisms. The ACL (Access Control List) system introduced in Redis 6 enables administrators to define fine-grained user permissions, thereby restricting which commands and keys each user can access. Through the ACL framework, every access can be linked to a specific authenticated principal, facilitating detailed accountability.

Monitoring access further involves capturing command execution details including the timestamp, user identity, client IP, and command arguments. Native Redis logging via the MONITOR command streams every command received by the Redis server, enabling external capture and archival of real-time operations. While MONITOR is invaluable for investigative purposes, it is resource-intensive and unsuitable for production use when continuous auditing is required. Instead, production systems implement selective logging mechanisms, for example, by intercepting commands at the proxy layer or enabling Redis keyspace notifications configured to emit events for specific operations on sensitive keys.

Redis's flexibility allows sensitive operations such as authentication attempts, configuration changes, and data modifications in critical keyspaces to be logged systematically. By combining the ACL system with command renaming, administrators can neutralize risky commands or substitute them with wrappers that log usage before executing the native function.

A common practice is to deploy a Redis proxy or middleware equipped with logging capabilities. This middleware intercepts client commands and produces structured audit entries, enriched with contextual metadata including client IP, execution time, command duration, and outcome status. Such logs are typically encoded in JSON or other parseable formats to ensure compatibility with Security Information and Event Management (SIEM) systems.

Redis keyspace notifications, which generate events on key modifications, are instrumental for logging data changes. Enabling notifications for commands like SET, DEL, or HSET over designated key patterns allows the audit subsystem to monitor critical keyspaces selectively. These events can then be consumed asynchronously by auditing daemons or analysts to reconstruct data alteration timelines.

Generating compliance-ready reports from auditing data requires systematic aggregation and correlation of logs generated by the techniques described above. To achieve this, organizations often integrate Redis audit logs with centralized log management and analytics platforms.

An effective reporting pipeline includes:

- **Log Collection:** Integration with tools such as Fluentd, Logstash, or custom collectors that consume Redis audit logs from files, syslog, or messaging queues.

- **Data Normalization:** Parsing and structuring log data to comply with standardized schemas like the Common Event Format (CEF) or JSON-based schemas preserves semantic consistency across heterogeneous sources.

- **Correlation and Enrichment:** Cross-referencing Redis logs with other system events, user directories, and IP intelligence to enhance the quality of audit data.

- **Report Templates:** Predefined templates aligning with regulatory criteria (e.g., PCI-DSS, HIPAA, GDPR) that identify access violations, suspicious activity patterns, or policy infractions.

Through this pipeline, compliance officers can extract actionable insights, such as identifying unauthorized access attempts, detecting anomalous command usage, or verifying data modification authenticity. Automating report generation helps maintain continuous compliance posture and facilitates auditing scopes during regulatory inspections.

Customization of Redis auditing to satisfy regulatory standards requires balancing comprehensiveness, performance, and data privacy. Critical considerations include:

- **Audit Scope Definition:** Precisely selecting keys, command subsets, and user groups for auditing avoids excess data collection and limits exposure.

- **Data Retention Policies:** Complying with mandates for data storage duration necessitates secure archival solutions and automated log rotation.

- **Anonymization and Encryption:** Sensitive audit logs may require cryptographic techniques to protect personally identifiable information (PII) and maintain confidentiality.

- **Integrity and Non-repudiation:** Employing log signing or append-only immutable stores guarantees that audit trails remain tamper-proof and verifiable.

- **Performance Optimization:** Leveraging asynchronous log export and batching prevents audit overhead from impairing Redis performance.

An example of configuring keyspace notifications selectively for auditing sensitive keys is as follows:

```
# Enable notifications for set and delete commands on hash keys
    starting with 'user:'
redis-cli config set notify-keyspace-events Ksh
```

The option string Ksh instructs Redis to notify on Keyspace events for string and hash data types, allowing integration with external listeners that capture and process these notifications for audit logging.

Redis auditing infrastructure is vital in forensic investigations and ongoing governance workflows. During incident investigations, detailed audit logs can reconstruct the sequence of actions leading to an anomaly or breach. This capability supports root cause analysis, evidence collection, and regulatory reporting.

For governance, continuous audit monitoring combined with alerting mechanisms enables rapid detection of policy violations. For instance, detecting repeated access denials, configuration changes, or mass deletions within restricted domains may trigger alerts to security teams.

Effective audit integration also involves role-based access to audit logs themselves, ensuring that only authorized personnel can view or manipulate audit records, thus preserving chain-of-custody integrity.

Redis's modular auditing framework, when appropriately tuned, provides indispensable tools to meet regulatory demands, support investigative processes, and establish rigorous data governance regimes in complex enterprise environments.

Chapter 7

Redis in Modern Application Architectures

Redis isn't just a high-speed database—it's a foundational pillar for contemporary, distributed application design. In this chapter, venture beyond basic cache use and discover how Redis empowers microservices, real-time systems, and highly interactive cloud applications. Through practical examples and proven patterns, uncover ways to harness Redis for service discovery, coordination, and state management in today's most dynamic software environments.

7.1. Microservices and Service Discovery

Microservice architectures demand efficient, low-latency mechanisms for service registration, discovery, and status monitoring to maintain high availability and fault tolerance. Redis, with its exceptional in-memory speed and versatile data structures, provides an ideal backbone for managing these coordination tasks within a distributed ecosystem. Its ability to serve as a centralized yet highly performant state store enables microservices to dynamically register themselves, discover peers, and track operational statuses in real time.

At the core of Redis-based service discovery is the use of easily accessible, flexible data types such as hashes, sets, sorted sets, and streams, which can model service metadata and state effectively. Service registration typically involves writing an entry keyed by service name and instance identifier, frequently accompanied by associated metadata including IP address, port, version, or health check tokens. For example, a hash can maintain the current attributes of each instance, while a sorted set indexed by timestamps or priorities can facilitate selection among multiple replicas.

Redis's built-in expiration (TTL) feature is essential in managing service liveness, allowing automatic removal of stale entries when a microservice fails to renew its lease. This prevents clients from obtaining stale or unreachable endpoints, maintaining consistent and robust discovery semantics without heavy coordination or locking overhead. Heartbeat patterns implemented as periodic key refreshes provide a lightweight and resilient approach to status tracking.

A common design pattern involves service instances registering themselves under a key structure such as:

```
services:<service_name>:<instance_id>
```

with metadata stored as a hash and TTL managing instance validity. Service clients query the registry keys under the prefix `services:<service_name>:*` to retrieve active endpoints. This can be augmented with sorted sets to include load metrics or instance priorities, enabling intelligent client-side load balancing.

Additionally, Redis Pub/Sub channels facilitate event-driven update propagation across the microservices ecosystem. Upon registration, deregistration, or status change, a microservice can publish messages to dedicated channels, allowing subscribers to update caches or take reactive measures without polling. This pattern dramatically reduces network overhead and accelerates system-wide state convergence.

To illustrate, consider a scenario where a service instance performs its registration and heartbeat renewal as follows:

```python
import redis
import time

r = redis.Redis()

service_name = "auth_service"
instance_id = "auth_service_001"
service_key = f"services:{service_name}:{instance_id}"
metadata = {
    "ip": "10.0.0.5",
    "port": "8080",
    "version": "1.0.2"
}

def register_service():
    r.hset(service_key, mapping=metadata)
    r.expire(service_key, 30)
    r.publish(f"service_changes:{service_name}", f"REGISTER {
    instance_id}")

def heartbeat():
    r.expire(service_key, 30)

register_service()
while True:
    heartbeat()
    time.sleep(10)
```

This code snippet encapsulates a simplified yet effective registration and heartbeat renewal pattern. The TTL of 30 seconds ensures automatic expiry if the instance becomes unreachable, and publish-subscribe notifications propagate state changes throughout the microservice network.

Another critical design consideration is achieving high availability of the Redis infrastructure itself. Leveraging Redis Sentinel or Redis Cluster configurations ensures resilience, fault tolerance, and scalability, which are indispensable for mission-critical microservices. Sentinel provides automatic failover and monitoring, while Redis Cluster enables sharding and horizontal scalability, allowing the service registry to grow seamlessly with the system.

To reduce lookup latency and improve fault tolerance further, caching layers utilizing Redis can store recent lookup results with short TTLs, diminishing repeated Redis queries under high load. Additionally, clients can adopt local caches updated via Pub/Sub notifications to maintain near real-time knowledge of the service topology without overwhelming the central Redis instance.

Service discovery flows generally follow this sequence:

- Microservice instance registers itself with associated metadata and sets a TTL.

- The instance periodically renews the TTL (heartbeat).

- Clients query Redis for currently active instances under the service name prefix.

- Clients optionally subscribe to service change channels to receive notifications.

- On termination or failure (TTL expiry), Redis removes the service entry automatically.

This architecture provides strict consistency in the registry while retaining responsiveness due to Redis's in-memory design. Compared to DNS-based or heavyweight service discovery systems, Redis combines simplicity with speed and flexibility, supporting diverse operational patterns including blue-green deployments, canary releases, and dynamic scaling.

Redis enables microservice ecosystems to implement a robust, highly available service discovery and status tracking system by capitalizing on its in-memory data structures, TTL semantics, and event pub/sub mechanisms. Its integration as a fast, consistent backend supports low-latency coordination across microservices, ensuring real-time visibility and resilience in distributed environments. Designing service registration and discovery around these Redis capabilities fosters scalable, maintainable microservices architectures capable of meeting demanding production workloads.

7.2. Caching Strategies

Caching strategies constitute a critical component in optimizing system performance, particularly in data-intensive applications requiring low latency and high throughput. Redis, as an in-memory data structure store, offers flexible caching models that can significantly accelerate database performance and ensure cache coherence in distributed environments. The principal caching approaches enabled by Redis include cache-aside, write-back, write-through, and hybrid models, each tailoring data consistency and system responsiveness to varying operational requirements.

The *cache-aside* strategy, often known as lazy loading, is the most widely adopted approach to integrating Redis as a cache layer. In this paradigm, the application is responsible for explicitly loading data into the cache on demand. When a cache miss occurs, the application fetches the data from the primary database, caches it in Redis, and subsequently serves requests from the cache until eviction or invalidation. This method excels in read-heavy workloads where data freshness can be moderately relaxed. Cache-aside is particularly effective at reducing the load on backend databases by preventing redundant read operations, thereby improving response times and throughput.

The implementation of cache-aside requires careful management of cache invalidation and miss handling to avoid stale data or cache inconsistencies. A typical sequence for a read request is:

```
def get_data(key):
    value = redis.get(key)
    if value is None:
        value = database.fetch(key)
        if value:
            redis.set(key, value)
    return value
```

In this model, writes are directed exclusively to the primary database, and the cache is updated or invalidated asynchronously, usually via explicit eviction commands or time-to-live (TTL) settings. While this simplifies cache coherence, it introduces potential latency during cache misses and requires the application to handle fallback accesses gracefully.

Contrastingly, the *write-through* caching strategy enforces synchronous updates between the cache and the backing store. Every write operation is first propagated to Redis and then simultaneously or subsequently persisted in the database. This approach guarantees data consistency between the cache and the database, effectively eliminating stale reads. Write-through caching is advantageous in scenarios where data durability and coherence are paramount but can introduce additional write latency due to synchronous database commits.

A canonical write-through pattern adapts the write path as shown:

```
def set_data(key, value):
    redis.set(key, value)
    database.update(key, value)
```

One caveat in write-through caching is the risk of cascading failures or bottlenecks if the database becomes slow or unavailable, as cache writes depend on successful backend updates. To mitigate this, Redis can be used with replication and fast failover capabilities, ensuring high availability of cache data even during transient database outages.

The *write-back* strategy, also termed write-behind, differs by updating the cache first and deferring database writes asynchronously. This approach reduces write latency, as the application only waits for the cache operation to complete. Additionally, it enables efficient batching of write operations to the database, improving throughput especially in high-volume write scenarios. However, it introduces complexity in maintaining data durability and consistency, demanding mechanisms to buffer and flush modified cache entries reliably.

Implementing write-back caching with Redis typically involves internal queues or Redis streams to accumulate updates before committing them in bulk to the database, as exemplified below:

```
def set_data_write_back(key, value):
    redis.set(key, value)
    redis.lpush('write_queue', (key, value))

def flush_write_queue():
    while redis.llen('write_queue') > 0:
        (key, value) = redis.rpop('write_queue')
        database.update(key, value)
```

Proper handling of failure scenarios, such as system crashes before database synchronization, is essential to prevent data loss. Logging, replication, and periodic persistence checkpoints are necessary components complementing write-back strategies.

Hybrid caching models integrate aspects of the aforementioned strategies to leverage their respective strengths. For instance, a system may adopt cache-aside for read operations to minimize cache pollution and write-through for critical updates requiring immediate consistency. Alternatively, a tiered caching architecture may employ write-back in intermediate Redis layers with eventual synchronization to persistent databases, combining low latency and high data durability.

Across distributed systems, ensuring cache coherence—a consistent view of data in multiple cache nodes—remains challenging. Redis Cluster supports sharding, enabling horizontal scaling, but introduces complexities in synchronizing data states. Techniques such as cache versioning, atomic operations via Lua scripting, and leveraging Redis's Pub/Sub or Keyspace Notifications facilitate co-ordinated cache invalidation and update broadcasting to maintain coherence. For example, propagation of cache invalidation messages across nodes ensures stale entries are purged promptly, enhancing data consistency.

Latency reduction through Redis caching stems from its in-memory storage and optimized data structures, enabling sub-millisecond retrieval. By offloading repetitive and read-intensive queries from slower disk-based databases, Redis allows rapid response cycles and supports higher concurrent user loads. Modern Redis deployments complement caching with persistence options like RDB snapshots and AOF logs to balance performance with data safety.

Selecting an appropriate caching strategy with Redis involves trade-offs between latency, consistency, and complexity. Cache-aside suits systems prioritizing read scalability and eventual consistency; write-through enforces strong consistency at the cost of write latency; write-back maximizes write throughput with deferred persistence risks. Hybrid models and distributed coordination mechanisms provide flexible adaptations to specific application domains and operational constraints, solidifying Redis as a versatile caching platform in modern architectures.

7.3. Event-Driven and Real-Time Systems

Scalable event processing lies at the core of building responsive and efficient real-time applications. Redis, with its versatile data structures and PUB/SUB and Streams APIs, provides a robust foundation for architecting systems that handle event-driven workloads with low latency and high throughput. This section explores how Redis enables diverse event processing pipelines, from simple notification services to complex analytics workflows, emphasizing architectural patterns and practical design considerations.

Redis' PUB/SUB (publish/subscribe) mechanism offers a straight-forward, lightweight messaging pattern suited for scenarios requiring transient event dissemination without persistence. Publishers send messages to named channels, while subscribers receive those messages in real time if connected at the time of publishing. This method is inherently scalable: Redis distributes messages to all subscribed clients with minimal overhead, ensuring low-latency delivery. However, PUB/SUB does not provide message durability or guaranteed delivery; if clients disconnect or experience network issues, messages published during the downtime are lost. Consequently, PUB/SUB is ideal for ephemeral notifications, live updates (e.g., chat applications, gaming leaderboards), and real-time streaming data where occasional message loss is tolerable.

The emergence of Redis Streams dramatically expands Redis' capability to support event-driven architectures requiring reliable, durable event logs. A Redis Stream is a log data structure that stores messages (entries) with unique, time-ordered IDs. Producers append entries to streams, while consumer groups enable multiple clients to process events cooperatively or independently. Streams maintain history and support message acknowledgment, facilitating end-to-end delivery guarantees, retry mechanisms, and replayability-properties essential for mission-critical real-time workflows.

Architecturally, using Redis Streams enables an event-driven pipeline with the following components:

- **Producers**, or event emitters, append events to one or more Redis Streams, capturing state changes, user interactions, IoT sensor data, or other event sources.

- **Streams** serve as durable event logs, maintaining a persistent, ordered sequence of events in memory, with configurable retention and trimming policies.

- **Consumers** are organized as consumer groups, which distribute the workload of processing events among multiple clients. Each consumer receives distinct events, acknowledges processing success, and can claim unprocessed events from failed consumers, enabling fault tolerance and load balancing.

- **Processing nodes** transform, aggregate, or forward events downstream, including writing results to databases, updating caches, or triggering additional asynchronous actions.

The combination of message durability, consumer groups, and message acknowledgment enables building robust pipelines for real-time analytics and monitoring applications. The ability to replay events from streams supports state reconstruction and debugging capabilities crucial for complex event processing workflows.

The design of such pipelines often incorporates a layered approach. Typically, an ingestion layer captures high-velocity incoming events using streams with minimal latency. This layer funnels data into a processing layer that performs computational transformations or enrichments, possibly using Redis' Lua scripting or external stream processors consuming from Redis Streams. A final output layer may then push transformed events into notification services (e.g., via PUB/SUB), databases, or dashboards, enabling real-time insights and decision-making.

For example, consider a real-time fraud detection system for financial transactions. Transaction processing systems produce events appended to Redis Streams. A consumer group of processors evaluates each transaction against fraud detection rules. Matching events trigger updates stored in Redis hashes and alerts published via PUB/SUB channels to client dashboards. The persistent event log in Redis Streams facilitates comprehensive auditing and retrospective analysis, even during system failures.

Latency optimization in such event-driven architectures requires careful tuning of Redis configurations (e.g., maxmemory policies, stream retention limits) and network settings to sustain high event throughput and low processing delays. Horizontal scaling is achievable by deploying multiple Redis instances partitioned by streams or sharded keys, combined with strategically designed consumer groups to distribute workload evenly.

Redis Streams' rich feature set supports complex event-driven use cases beyond simple message passing:

- **Event sourcing**: capturing system state changes as immutable streams, enabling audit trails and state reconstruction.

- **CQRS (Command Query Responsibility Segregation)**: commanding changes via streams and servicing queries from up-to-date projections maintained asynchronously.

- **Workflow orchestration**: modeling multi-step processes where events trigger subsequent actions, with Redis tracking event states and dependencies.

Integration with popular streaming ecosystems, such as Apache Kafka or Apache Flink, extends Redis Streams as a complementary low-latency cache and event broker. In such hybrid architectures, Redis handles quick, near-instantaneous processing close to the application, while big-data systems manage long-term storage and complex analytics.

Redis provides a versatile platform for building scalable event-driven systems. The PUB/SUB mechanism excels in lightweight, transient notification scenarios demanding minimal overhead and immediate message delivery. Redis Streams' durability, consumer groups, and message persistence enable mission-critical pipelines that require resilience, reliability, and sophisticated processing semantics. Leveraging these Redis capabilities, developers can construct highly responsive real-time applications ranging from simple live notifications to advanced analytics workflows demanding fault tolerance and event replayability.

7.4. Session Management and User State

Managing user sessions and state in highly concurrent web and mobile applications presents considerable challenges, particularly when targeting global user bases with stringent consistency, scalability, and fault tolerance requirements. Central to designing effective session management systems is the choice and architecture of session storage models, which determine how user state is stored, retrieved, and synchronized across distributed components.

There are primarily three architectural paradigms for session storage: *in-memory session stores*, *distributed cache-backed stores*, and *database-backed session persistence*. Each of these exhibits distinct trade-offs in terms of latency, scalability, and consistency guarantees.

In-Memory Session Stores

In-memory solutions such as local server RAM or embedded caches provide the lowest latency access to session data. However, they are inherently limited by the server's memory capacity and challenges in horizontal scaling. For clustered environments, in-memory session replication protocols (e.g., using algorithms inspired by the *primary-backup* model) can be implemented, yet these often come at the cost of increased network overhead and complex synchronization logic, especially under high concurrency.

While suitable for scenarios where session affinity (sticky sessions) can be guaranteed-often via load balancer configurations-these approaches risk session loss upon server failures or redeployments, making them less attractive for global services requiring robust fault tolerance.

Distributed Cache-Backed Session Stores

Distributed caching systems such as Redis, Memcached, and Hazelcast have become the de facto standard for scalable, fault-tolerant session management. They support session data replication, sharding, and eviction policies to handle massive concurrent loads efficiently. Key features promoting their adoption include configurable persistence, multi-region availability, and support for atomic operations enabling strong consistency semantics.

Adopting Redis as an example, sessions can be stored as hash structures keyed by user session identifiers with fields representing user attributes, authentication tokens, or application-specific state. Advanced capabilities like Redis transactions (MULTI/EXEC) or Lua scripting allow atomic session updates, critical to preventing race conditions during concurrent session modifications.

From a scalability perspective, sharding session data across multiple cache nodes allows horizontal scaling to handle millions of simultaneous sessions. Replication and persistence options safeguard against data loss, providing eventual or strong consistency depending on configuration.

Database-Backed Session Persistence

Persistent storage in relational or NoSQL databases offers strong durability guarantees and complex query capabilities for session data analysis and auditing. However, the increased latency and throughput constraints necessitate caching layers or asynchronous mechanisms to prevent bottlenecks in user experience.

Databases such as Cassandra, DynamoDB, or PostgreSQL can handle massive concurrent writes and reads if designed correctly, though schemata must be optimized for session retrieval patterns, typically indexed by session IDs and expiration timestamps.

Global User Base Considerations

Global-scale applications must address latency distribution and disaster recovery through multi-region session storage architectures. Strategies include:

1. **Geo-Partitioned Session Stores**: Sessions are pinned to the region closest to the user to minimize access latency. Data synchronization across regions occurs asynchronously to preserve availability but may introduce eventual consistency challenges.

2. **Globally Distributed Datastores**: Systems like *Cloud Spanner* or *Couchbase* offer strong consistency across regions at the cost of increased write latencies, suitable for scenarios where session state correctness is paramount.

3. **Hybrid Models**: Combining local caches with periodic global synchronization balances latency and consistency, often supported by Conflict-Free Replicated Data Types (CRDTs) to resolve divergent session state conflicts automatically.

Practical Recipes for Session Invalidation and User Tracking

To maintain data integrity and secure user state, session invalidation strategies are essential, particularly on user logout, session expiration, or credential revocation events.

A practical recipe for session invalidation in distributed cache-backed models involves storing a session version or token timestamp that is compared against a centralized revocation or blacklist store. Upon invalidation, the session token is marked as expired, and subsequent requests trigger forced re-authentication.

Implementing sliding session expiration reduces state loss by extending session TTL (time-to-live) on active user interactions. This can be achieved by renewing the key expiration atomically within each valid request processing, ensuring active sessions persist while dormant ones expire promptly.

User tracking benefits from session metadata enrichment, logging user activity, client device identifiers, IP addresses, and geolocation data within session stores. This supports anomaly detection, personalization, and analytics without coupling tightly to the primary user database.

Minimizing State Loss in High-Concurrency Environments

To prevent session state loss during server failures, network partitions, or concurrent updates, several design patterns and best practices are recommended:

- **Atomic Session Updates**: Use atomic operations or transactions in the session store to guard against interleaved modifications causing inconsistent state.

- **Idempotent Session Mutations**: Design session updates to be repeatable without side effects, facilitating safe retries in case of communication failures.

- **Session Replication and Persistence**: Employ replication and persistent backing stores to recover session data after node failures.

- **Graceful Session Expiration**: Implement mechanisms to handle session expiration gracefully, allowing client applications to detect and recover user state without abrupt termination.

Example: Redis-Based Session Storage

The following Lua script demonstrates an atomic operation to extend a session TTL while updating an access timestamp, ensuring minimal session loss and synchronized expiration in a Redis-backed environment:

```
local sessionKey = KEYS[1]
local ttl = tonumber(ARGV[1])
local accessTime = ARGV[2]

if redis.call("EXISTS", sessionKey) == 1 then
  redis.call("HSET", sessionKey, "last_access", accessTime)
  redis.call("EXPIRE", sessionKey, ttl)
  return 1
else
  return 0
end
```

In this routine, the session's existence is verified atomically; if present, the last access time is updated and expiration renewed. This pattern supports sliding session expiration under concurrent access while minimizing state loss.

Effective session management in high-concurrency, globally distributed environments demands a balanced approach incorporating distributed caching layers, persistent storage, and targeted invalidation strategies. Architectures must support strong consistency where necessary, while enabling low-latency access for enhanced user experience. The integration of atomic session operations, multi-region deployment strategies, and adaptive expiration policies are essential components mastering user state handling at scale.

7.5. Distributed Locking and Coordination

Distributed systems inherently require mechanisms to coordinate access to shared resources and ensure consistency across multiple nodes. Redis, a widely adopted in-memory data store, offers primitives that facilitate distributed locking, semaphores, and leader election. These coordination patterns are fundamental for maintaining consistency and availability in mission-critical, multi-node deployments. This section examines robust approaches to implementing distributed locks and semaphores in Redis, explores leader election algorithms, and discusses the associated pitfalls and best practices to guarantee safety and liveness.

Distributed Locks Using Redis

A distributed lock ensures exclusive access to a shared resource by permitting only one process at a time to hold the lock. In Redis, the simplest lock can be implemented via the SET command with the NX (set if not exists) and PX (expiry in milliseconds) options:

```
SET resource_name unique_lock_id NX PX 30000
```

Here, resource_name is the lock key, unique_lock_id is a client-generated identifier, and the expiry safeguards against deadlocks caused by client failures.

Correctness Considerations

Robust distributed locking requires satisfaction of two properties:

- **Safety (Mutual Exclusion)**: At most one client can hold the lock at any time.

- **Liveness (Deadlock Freedom)**: The system guarantees eventual progress; no client waits indefinitely.

The atomic SET NX PX command helps mitigate race conditions in lock acquisition. However, correctness issues arise if clients fail or network partitions occur. For example, if the client holding the lock experiences a pause longer than the expiry, the lock may be erroneously acquired by another client, potentially violating mutual exclusion.

Renewing and Releasing Locks

Since Redis locks have finite TTL, applications frequently implement a lock renewal mechanism prior to expiry. Renewals must be conditional on the lock still being held, verified by matching the unique lock identifier to prevent clients from mistakenly extending locks they do not own.

Releasing a lock must be atomic and conditional: only the client that owns the lock should delete it. This is typically implemented as a Lua script to ensure atomicity:

```
if redis.call("GET", KEYS[1]) == ARGV[1] then
    return redis.call("DEL", KEYS[1])
else
    return 0
end
```

This script checks if the lock's value matches the caller's identifier before deleting the key.

Redlock Algorithm

To increase safety and fault tolerance in distributed environments, the *Redlock* algorithm coordinates lock acquisition on multiple independent Redis instances. A client attempts to acquire a lock on the majority of Redis nodes within a time constraint, acquires the lock only if it succeeds on a quorum before expiry, and releases all locks upon completion.

Despite some debate in the research community, Redlock can provide stronger safety guarantees by mitigating risks arising from single-node failures and network partitions, provided the instances do not share common points of failure.

Distributed Semaphores

Semaphores generalize locks by allowing a specified number of clients to concurrently acquire permission to access a resource. Implementing a semaphore in Redis requires careful state management to maintain a count of active holders without race conditions.

A common pattern utilizes a sorted set where each client adds an entry representing a semaphore slot with its unique token and timestamp. Acquisition succeeds only if the number of current holders is below the semaphore capacity, coupled with expiry pruning to recycle stale entries.

```
local key = KEYS[1]
local limit = tonumber(ARGV[1])
local now = tonumber(ARGV[2])
local token = ARGV[3]
-- Remove expired entries
redis.call("ZREMRANGEBYSCORE", key, "-inf", now - 30000)
local count = redis.call("ZCARD", key)
if count < limit then
    redis.call("ZADD", key, now, token)
    return 1
else
    return 0
end
```

This script ensures that only the allowed number of clients hold the semaphore simultaneously, and expired tokens are removed to prevent deadlocks.

Challenges in Semaphore Use

Semaphores require client coordination to renew or release their tokens timely. Failure to do so may cause resource starvation or inflated semaphore counts, breaking liveness guarantees. Implementations must carefully tune expiry durations and handle client crashes gracefully.

Leader Election Algorithms

Leader election is critical in distributed systems to designate a single node responsible for coordination tasks, such as scheduling or configuration management.

Simple Leader Election with Redis Keys

A simple pattern uses a Redis key as a leadership token. Nodes attempt to acquire the leadership lock via the SET NX PX command, using unique identifiers. The current leader must renew the lock within the TTL to maintain leadership. Upon failure, another node can acquire the lock and assume leadership.

Ensuring Stability and Avoiding Split-Brain

Leader election must avoid split-brain scenarios-multiple nodes simultaneously believing they are the leader-resulting in inconsistent system states. This risk arises if clock drift or network delays cause lock expirations and overlapping leadership claims.

To mitigate split-brain, leader election mechanisms can:

- Use sufficiently long TTLs relative to expected pause durations.

- Perform leadership transfer only after explicit detection of leader failure.

- Employ the Redlock algorithm for multi-instance quorum-based leader election.

- Combine Redis coordination with external consensus systems (e.g., ZooKeeper, etcd) in highly critical systems.

Pitfalls and Best Practices

Expiry and Clock Drift

TTL-based locks depend on synchronized clocks or bounded execution delays for safety. Clock drift or long client pauses can cause expiry before operation completion. Use monotonic clocks where possible and tune expiry conservatively.

Non-Idempotent Lock Usage

Operations guarded by locks must be idempotent or restartable because lock expiry can cause repetition or concurrent execution in failure cases.

Avoiding Deadlocks

Implementing timeouts and automatic expiry prevents indefinite lock holding due to client failure. Ensure lock renewal protocols are robust and that distributed semaphores prune expired entries.

Use of Lua Scripts

Atomicity of complex lock and semaphore operations should be ensured through Redis Lua scripts to avoid race conditions between multiple commands.

Monitoring and Observability

Deploy monitoring of lock durations, failure rates, and lease renewals to detect potential anomalies and prevent system-wide stalls.

Distributed locking and coordination in Redis hinge upon atomic operations, strict ownership guarantees, expiry management, and careful client cooperation. Frameworks like Redlock bolster safety by leveraging consensus across multiple Redis nodes. Semaphores and leader election patterns further support scalability and fault tolerance. Due diligence in clock synchronization, expiry tuning, and fault handling is essential to preserve safety and liveness in mission-critical deployments.

These patterns form the backbone of resilient, coherent distributed applications powered by Redis orchestration capabilities, supporting scalability and robustness under concurrent multi-node workloads.

7.6. Rate Limiting and Throttling

Managing the flow of requests to APIs and services is critical for maintaining system stability, ensuring equitable resource usage, and mitigating abuse. Redis, with its in-memory data structures and atomic commands, offers a versatile foundation for implementing robust rate limiting and throttling mechanisms. This section explores Redis-based solutions grounded in the token bucket and leaky bucket algorithms, outlining their operational principles, atomicity guarantees, and practical deployment in high-traffic environments.

At the core of rate limiting is the enforcement of policy constraints that restrict the number of operations a client can perform in a defined time window. Both token bucket and leaky bucket algorithms achieve this by controlling the availability of permits for request processing, albeit via different paradigms.

Token Bucket Algorithm in Redis

The token bucket algorithm defines a bucket with a fixed maximum capacity and a refill rate at which tokens are added. Each incoming request consumes one token. If tokens are available, the request proceeds; otherwise, it is rejected or delayed. This model allows for burstiness up to the bucket capacity, accommodating variable request rates while ensuring long-term rate compliance.

Implementing this in Redis leverages its atomic operations like INCRBY, GET, and Lua scripting to maintain counter integrity under concurrency. The bucket state is represented by a key containing the current token count and a timestamp of the last refill. On each request, a Lua script executes atomically to:

- Calculate elapsed time since the last refill.

- Compute tokens to add based on refill rate and elapsed time.

- Adjust the token count, capped at the bucket capacity.

- If tokens remain, decrement one token and allow the request.

- Otherwise, reject or throttle the request.

A typical Lua script snippet is:

```
local key = KEYS[1]
local capacity = tonumber(ARGV[1])
local refill_rate = tonumber(ARGV[2]) -- tokens per second
local now = tonumber(ARGV[3])

local data = redis.call('HMGET', key, 'tokens', 'timestamp')
local tokens = tonumber(data[1]) or capacity
```

```
local timestamp = tonumber(data[2]) or 0

local delta = math.max(0, now - timestamp)
local new_tokens = math.min(capacity, tokens + delta *
    refill_rate)

local allowed = 0
if new_tokens >= 1 then
  allowed = 1
  new_tokens = new_tokens - 1
end

redis.call('HMSET', key, 'tokens', new_tokens, 'timestamp', now)
redis.call('EXPIRE', key, math.ceil(capacity / refill_rate * 2))
return allowed
```

This script ensures atomic updates, avoiding race conditions in high-concurrency deployments. Expiration on the key prevents memory leakage when clients are inactive.

Leaky Bucket Algorithm in Redis

The leaky bucket algorithm conceptualizes a fixed-rate output leak from a bucket into which incoming requests arrive. It smooths burst traffic by queueing excess requests and processing them at a controlled, constant rate. Unlike the token bucket, which allows bursts within capacity, the leaky bucket enforces a strict average rate limit.

Redis implementations use a timestamp-based queue or a counter combined with timestamps. A common approach records the timestamp of the last allowed request and enforces spacing between allowed requests according to the leak rate.

The Lua script atomically:

- Reads the last request timestamp.

- Compares the current time against the allowed interval.

- If sufficient time has elapsed, updates the timestamp and allows the request.

171

- Otherwise, rejects or delays the request.

Example Lua logic:

```
local key = KEYS[1]
local interval = tonumber(ARGV[1]) -- in milliseconds
local now = tonumber(ARGV[2])

local last_time = tonumber(redis.call('GET', key)) or 0

if now - last_time >= interval then
  redis.call('SET', key, now, 'PX', interval * 2)
  return 1
else
  return 0
end
```

This method guarantees steady processing rates but may introduce increased latencies for bursty traffic.

Atomicity and Fairness Considerations

The atomic execution of Lua scripts in Redis ensures that concurrent requests do not produce inconsistent state or allow circumvention of limits. This atomicity is particularly crucial in high-traffic, distributed systems where race conditions can lead to over-allocation of tokens or allowance.

Fairness across multiple clients or resources is maintained by constructing key schemes that isolate rate limits per user token, IP address, or API key. Namespacing Redis keys, for example `rate:api_key`, supports granular control without cross-interference.

When operating across clustered Redis deployments, care must be taken with key distribution to avoid cross-node latency and inconsistencies. Choosing key hashes that guarantee co-location can facilitate atomic script execution.

Real-Time Enforcement and High Throughput Deployment

Redis's low latency and in-memory architecture enable real-time rate limit enforcement with minimal overhead. For systems processing tens or hundreds of thousands of requests per second, embedding rate limiting scripts within request processing pipelines provides immediate feedback on quota status, enabling adaptive backoff or error reporting.

To improve performance in extreme scenarios, batching rate limiting checks or deferring enforcement asynchronously may be considered, albeit at the cost of instantaneous accuracy.

Monitoring keys' time-to-live values and eviction patterns assists in tuning refill rates and bucket capacities to balance resource usage with protection efficacy.

Combining Rate Limiting with Abuse Protection

Integrating Redis-based rate limiting with abuse detection mechanisms, such as anomaly scoring or suspicious pattern detection, allows conditional adjustments of limits. Dynamic throttling schemes can tighten parameters for misbehaving clients or operate globally during attack periods.

Implementing cascading limits—combining short-term bursts with longer-term quotas—using multiple Redis keys and TTLs confers layered protection. For instance, a per-second token bucket restricts bursts, while a per-hour counter caps total usage.

Redis's flexibility permits the orchestration of these sophisticated schemes using Lua scripts that modify multiple keys transactionally, ensuring coherent enforcement.

Summary of Redis-Based Rate Limiting Advantages

Redis-powered rate limiting solutions excel in enabling:

- **Atomic updates** through Lua scripting, preventing state corruption under concurrency.

- **Flexible algorithms**, supporting both bursty and smooth traffic shaping via token and leaky bucket variants.

- **Fine-grained control** by scoping limits on various client or API identifiers.

- **Real-time enforcement** conducive to rapid client feedback and adaptive policies.

- **Scalability** leveraging Redis clustering and optimized key management.

In mission-critical, high-volume environments, adopting Redis-based rate limiting architectures ensures robustness, predictability, and fairness in API resource management.

Chapter 8

Integrations and Ecosystem

Redis's versatility shines brightest when seamlessly integrated within diverse technology landscapes. This chapter opens the door to Redis's vibrant ecosystem, revealing how it connects with everything from programming languages to cloud services, containers, and observability platforms. Journey through hands-on integration recipes and automation blueprints that transform Redis into the nerve center of modern data infrastructure.

8.1. Connecting from Diverse Programming Environments

The versatility of Redis as an in-memory data structure store is magnified by the breadth of client libraries that facilitate its integration across diverse programming environments. This section provides a comparative overview of popular Redis client libraries, focusing on their feature sets, performance considerations, and best practices essential for reliable and efficient connectivity in production scenarios. Particular emphasis is placed on error handling paradigms and connection pooling strategies, which are critical for maintaining robustness and throughput in real-world applications.

Redis client libraries exist for virtually all major programming languages, each with nuances shaped by language idioms, concurrency models, and ecosystem conventions. Among the most mature and widely adopted clients are redis-py for Python, Jedis and Lettuce for Java, Node-redis for JavaScript (Node.js), and hiredis for C/C++ with numerous bindings for other languages.

redis-py adopts a synchronous design by default but supports asynchronous operation via asyncio in recent versions. It offers comprehensive Redis command coverage, connection pooling, and robust error reporting aligned with Python's exception model. For Python developers, redis-py is the de facto standard, noted for clarity and ease of integration with web frameworks and data processing pipelines.

Jedis is a synchronous Java client that emphasizes simplicity and performance, suitable for applications favoring blocking calls and explicit resource management. **Lettuce**, on the other hand, provides a fully asynchronous, reactive API based on Netty, supporting multi-threaded and event-driven architectures. Lettuce's design allows scalable, high-throughput connectivity, with built-in support for pipelining, transactions, and pub/sub, making it well suited for modern concurrent Java applications.

Node-redis embodies event-driven, asynchronous interaction congruent with Node.js' single-threaded model. It supports promises and callbacks, allowing flexible asynchronous patterns. The client provides features essential to Node.js environments such as automatic reconnection, offline queueing, and extensible command definitions.

hiredis acts as a minimalistic, high-performance C client providing a fast protocol parser which can serve as the backend for bindings in higher-level languages. Its simplicity and speed come at the cost of limited direct abstraction, placing management responsibilities like connection pooling and retry strategies on the integrator.

When selecting a Redis client, critical criteria include:

- **Command Coverage:** Full support for Redis commands and data types, especially advanced features such as Streams, Geo, and modules.

- **Asynchronous Support:** Ability to utilize non-blocking calls, integral for scalable applications and event-driven architectures.

- **Connection Management:** Inclusion of robust connection pooling or multiplexing to optimize resource utilization.

- **Error Handling Frameworks:** Facilities for granular exception management and automatic recovery.

- **Performance Characteristics:** Latency overhead, throughput efficiency, and resource footprint under various load conditions.

Clients like Lettuce and Node-redis, emphasizing asynchronous operation, typically exhibit lower latencies in highly concurrent environments due to non-blocking I/O. Conversely, synchronous clients like Jedis provide simplicity and predictability in single-threaded or thread-isolated contexts.

Error handling is a foundational requirement for resilient Redis integration. Clients uniformly raise exceptions or error events for protocol errors, command syntax issues, or server-side failures. Beyond immediate errors, transient network faults such as timeouts, connection drops, or Redis server failovers necessitate built-in reconnection and retry mechanisms to sustain availability.

Best practices include:

- **Timeout Configuration:** Explicitly specify socket and command timeouts to avoid indefinite blocking.

- **Automatic Reconnection:** Utilize client capabilities to detect disconnections and transparently reconnect.

- **Idempotent Command Patterns:** Design application commands such that retries do not cause undesirable side effects.

- **Circuit Breakers and Backoff:** Implement retry logic that incorporates exponential backoff and jitter to prevent cascading failures.

- **Monitoring and Logging:** Instrument clients to emit diagnostic events capturing connection state transitions and errors.

`redis-py`, for example, raises `RedisError` or subclasses for Redis exceptions, while connection errors manifest as `ConnectionError`. Proper try-except constructs coupled with reconnection loops enable graceful degradation. Similarly, `Node-redis` emits `error` events on the client socket to which handlers can attach for recovery workflows.

Connection pooling fundamentally increases concurrency and resource efficiency by reusing established TCP connections rather than incurring overhead on each request. Most mature clients offer connection pool abstractions that manage a configurable pool of connections, incorporating thread-safe borrow/release semantics.

Consider the following exemplary Python snippet using `redis-py`'s connection pool:

```
import redis

pool = redis.ConnectionPool(host='localhost', port=6379,
    max_connections=10)
```

```
client = redis.Redis(connection_pool=pool)

result = client.get('key')
```

This approach ensures no more than ten simultaneous connections are established to Redis, allowing the client to queue commands internally if the pool is exhausted.

In asynchronous clients such as Lettuce, connection multiplexing over a single TCP connection is common, enabling concurrent command execution without dedicating multiple connections, thus reducing resource consumption while maintaining throughput.

Deploying Redis clients in production necessitates tailored tuning:

- **Pool Sizing:** Balance between concurrently active requests and Redis server's capacity. Oversized pools can strain server resources, while undersized pools can throttle application performance.

- **Latency Sensitivity:** For latency-critical applications, preferring asynchronous clients or multiplexed I/O can achieve minimal overhead.

- **Resource Limits and Cleanup:** Ensure clients release connections properly under error conditions and during shutdown.

- **Cluster and Sentinel Support:** Use clients that support Redis Cluster and Sentinel for high availability, automatic failover detection, and topology awareness.

- **Security Parameters:** Configure SSL/TLS connections, authentication tokens, and command whitelisting to maintain compliance and data integrity.

Effective error handling, combined with optimized connection management, maintains high availability and efficient resource use. Integration tests replicating failure modes and load testing under peak conditions are advisable to validate client and configuration choices prior to deployment.

Selecting and correctly configuring Redis client libraries across programming environments demands a nuanced understanding of application concurrency requirements, error management expectations, and operational contexts. Through deliberate adoption of client-specific best practices for pooling and fault tolerance, developers can leverage Redis's high performance potential while ensuring robust, reliable service integration.

8.2. Integration with Cloud Services

The deployment of Redis within modern cloud environments capitalizes on managed offerings, hybrid architectures, and serverless paradigms to deliver scalable, resilient, and highly available data platforms. Managed cloud services for Redis abstract away operational complexities, enabling organizations to integrate Redis as a core component within their cloud-native infrastructures with minimal administrative overhead. Simultaneously, hybrid models leverage Redis deployments both on-premises and in the cloud to address latency, compliance, and cost considerations, providing flexibility across diverse application landscapes.

- **Managed Redis Services**

  Major cloud providers offer fully managed Redis instances, such as Amazon ElastiCache for Redis, Microsoft Azure Cache for Redis, and Google Cloud Memorystore for Redis. These services automate provisioning, patching, backups, failover, and scaling, thus streamlining operational workflows. By offloading infrastructure management, development teams can focus on optimizing application logic and performance tuning.

From an architectural perspective, managed Redis offerings provide multi-availability zone replication, automatic failover, and data persistence configured out-of-the-box. These features cater to high availability and disaster recovery requirements. For latency-sensitive applications, providers also support cluster configurations and sharded Redis instances, facilitating horizontal scaling beyond single-node limitations.

Integration with cloud-native identity and access management systems ensures secure communications and controlled access. For example, Amazon ElastiCache integrates with AWS IAM and supports Virtual Private Cloud peering, enabling role-based access control within private networks. Such mechanisms are fundamental for maintaining stringent security postures.

- **Hybrid Deployment Models**

  The hybrid model incorporates Redis across on-premises data centers and public clouds, exploiting the strengths of each environment. This model is particularly relevant in scenarios demanding data locality, regulatory compliance, or predictable cost management. Hybrid deployments often employ a multi-region Redis setup, using tools like Redis Replication or Redis Enterprise to synchronize datasets between local and cloud-hosted nodes.

  Latency optimization is essential in hybrid configurations. Edge computing strategies may embed Redis at the network edge, close to data sources or end-users, to reduce round-trip times. Data synchronization between edge Redis instances and central cloud-hosted Redis deployments can be managed through asynchronous replication, minimizing impact on application responsiveness while ensuring eventual consistency.

  From a networking perspective, secure tunnels and private

connectivity options (e.g., AWS Direct Connect, Azure Ex-
pressRoute) enable reliable and encrypted communication
channels for Redis traffic between on-premises and cloud infrastructures.

- **Serverless Architectures and Redis**

  Redis functions as a pivotal state management and caching
  layer in serverless architectures. Serverless functions, char-
  acterized by ephemeral execution and statelessness, benefit
  greatly from Redis's low-latency, in-memory data access for
  session state, rate limiting, and event-driven workflows.

  Integration strategies involve deploying Redis in managed
  cloud services to provide persistent state behind event-
  triggered logic. For instance, a serverless function in AWS
  Lambda can access an ElastiCache Redis instance residing
  within a Virtual Private Cloud to perform atomic operations,
  such as incrementing counters or managing locks, critical
  to coordinating distributed processes without dedicated
  backend servers.

  Caching user authentication tokens or API response data in
  Redis reduces cold start latency that can otherwise degrade
  serverless performance. Additionally, Redis's support for
  data structures like streams and sorted sets facilitates task
  queues and time-series data ingestion in serverless pipelines,
  enabling complex event processing patterns.

  The auto-scaling nature of serverless environments necessitates dynamic Redis client connection management. Connection pooling and client-side retry logic mitigate connection
  overhead and transient network issues, maintaining operational efficiency under fluctuating loads.

- **Scaling and Operational Efficiency Through Cloud-
  Native Tools**

Cloud-native ecosystems offer orchestration and monitoring tools that enhance Redis integration. Kubernetes operators, such as the Redis Enterprise Operator or community-supported Redis Operators, automate deployment, scaling, failover, and backup workflows within container orchestration platforms. These operators leverage native constructs like StatefulSets and PersistentVolumes, ensuring Redis instances maintain data persistence while supporting rolling upgrades and self-healing capabilities.

Horizontal Pod Autoscalers and custom metrics sources can trigger elastically scaled Redis clusters in response to workload changes. For stateful Redis clusters, scaling must balance capacity adjustments with shard rebalancing, avoiding data unavailability during reconfiguration.

Infrastructure-as-Code frameworks (e.g., Terraform, Cloud-Formation, ARM templates) codify Redis provisioning alongside networking and security policies. This enables repeatable, auditable deployment processes fitting enterprise governance models.

Observability integrates Prometheus exporters and Grafana dashboards tailored for Redis metrics such as keyspace hits, memory usage, client connections, and slow commands. Real-time telemetry supports proactive anomaly detection and facilitates capacity planning, essential for maintaining high throughput and low latency.

Furthermore, cloud event-driven services like AWS Event-Bridge or Azure Event Grid can be combined with Redis streams to architect event-sourced systems where Redis acts as a durable queue, bridging ephemeral serverless functions with persistent application state.

The synergy between Redis and cloud services epitomizes the convergence of in-memory data processing with scalable, reliable, and secure infrastructure. Managed Redis services simplify operational burdens while hybrid deployments address complex enterprise requirements. Serverless architectures exploit Redis to manage ephemeral state and accelerate event processing. Finally, cloud-native orchestration and monitoring tools provide the mechanisms necessary for seamless scaling and operational excellence. Mastery of these integration strategies empowers architects to build resilient, high-performance applications optimized for the dynamic demands of contemporary cloud ecosystems.

8.3. Observability and Monitoring Ecosystem

Centralized observability pipelines are foundational to maintaining robust, scalable, and performant distributed systems. Integrating Redis within these pipelines enables enhanced visibility into data stores and caching layers, which are often critical performance bottlenecks and failure points. Redis emits rich telemetry data that, when properly captured and forwarded, enriches the monitoring context and accelerates troubleshooting. This section details the integration of Redis metrics and logs into popular observability platforms such as Prometheus, Grafana, and the ELK (Elasticsearch, Logstash, Kibana) stack, offering configuration guidance and architectural considerations to achieve end-to-end service visibility.

Redis natively exposes a wealth of metrics over its INFO command interface, including statistics about commands, memory usage, clients, replication, and persistence. To incorporate these into a centralized monitoring pipeline, exporters act as intermediaries that poll Redis and translate its raw data into formats consumable by observability tools.

Prometheus Exporter Configuration

The redis_exporter is the de-facto standard for exporting Redis metrics to Prometheus. It periodically queries Redis via the INFO

command and converts the results into Prometheus-compatible
metrics exposed over HTTP.

```
redis_exporter --redis.addr=redis://localhost:6379 \
               --web.listen-address=":9121"
```

Prometheus scrapes the exporter endpoint as part of its service discovery configuration:

```
scrape_configs:
  - job_name: 'redis'
    static_configs:
      - targets: ['localhost:9121']
```

Key configuration parameters to tune in production include the
scrape interval (default 15s) and Redis authentication credentials,
which can be securely injected via environment variables or configuration files.

Custom Exporters and Metric Augmentation

In scenarios requiring extended observability such as capturing latency percentiles, keyspace notification events, or Lua script execution times, a custom exporter or additional instrumentation layers may be necessary. These custom agents can leverage the Redis
MONITOR command or Redis modules with telemetry support, exporting enriched metrics to Prometheus or pushing them directly
into an intermediary time-series database.

Redis logs provide operational context vital for diagnosing errors,
slow commands, and connection issues. Centralizing logs alongside metrics enhances root cause analysis and anomaly detection.

Logstash Pipeline Integration

The ELK stack, particularly with Logstash, is commonly employed
for collecting and parsing Redis logs. Redis can be configured to
write logs either to a file or syslog:

```
loglevel notice
logfile "/var/log/redis/redis-server.log"
```

A typical Logstash pipeline for Redis logs uses the `file` input plugin, combined with grok and date filters to parse timestamps and categorize log levels:

```
input {
  file {
    path => "/var/log/redis/redis-server.log"
    start_position => "beginning"
  }
}
filter {
  grok {
    match => { "message" => "\[%{TIMESTAMP_ISO8601:timestamp}\]
      %{LOGLEVEL:level} %{GREEDYDATA:message}" }
  }
  date {
    match => ["timestamp", "ISO8601"]
  }
}
output {
  elasticsearch {
    hosts => ["http://elasticsearch:9200"]
    index => "redis-logs-%{+YYYY.MM.dd}"
  }
}
```

Log Correlation Strategies

Integrating Redis logs with application and infrastructure logs in the ELK stack facilitates cross-layer correlation. Employing consistent request identifiers or tracing IDs within logs supports tracing request flows through cache tiers, improving the ability to connect latency spikes or errors seen in Redis metrics with specific client requests or backend faults.

Visual dashboards unify data into actionable insights. Grafana remains the most widely adopted frontend for Prometheus metrics and offers flexible integration with Elasticsearch as well.

Grafana Dashboards

Numerous community-supported Grafana dashboards for Redis are available, providing real-time views into key metrics such as memory fragmentation, commands processed, key expiration rates, and replication health. Custom dashboards can be con-

186

structed by importing Prometheus queries directly or connecting to Elasticsearch log indices.

An example Prometheus query showing Redis command processing rate:

```
rate(redis_commands_processed_total[1m])
```

This metric, visualized alongside latency percentiles and client connection counts, yields a multi-dimensional perspective on Redis operation health.

Alerts and Anomaly Detection

Both Prometheus Alertmanager and Kibana Alerting facilitate the definition of thresholds and anomaly detection rules on Redis metrics and logs, triggering notifications through email or integration with incident management systems. Effective alerting rules should combine multiple signals, such as increased slow commands count concurrent with memory usage approaching thresholds, to reduce false positives.

A typical architecture for comprehensive Redis observability integrates the elements as follows:

- Redis servers expose metrics via `redis_exporter` to Prometheus.

- Redis logs stream into Logstash, which parses and forwards them to Elasticsearch.

- Prometheus and Elasticsearch serve as data sources for Grafana dashboards.

- Correlation identifiers propagate through application logs and Redis logs to enable joined analysis.

- Alerting frameworks monitor both metrics and logs for rapid incident detection.

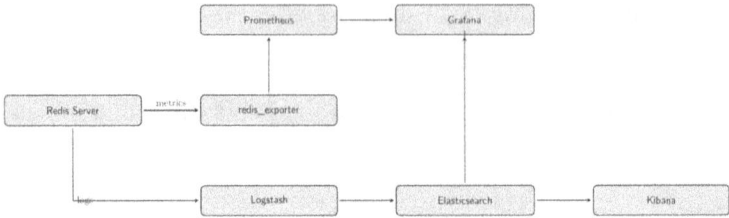

This architecture emphasizes modularity, allowing components such as exporters, log processors, or visualization tools to be substituted or scaled independently. Secure communication channels, authentication mechanisms, and data retention policies must be defined to comply with organizational requirements.

Polling Redis frequently can introduce measurable load, especially in clusters with many nodes. Setting appropriate scrape intervals and leveraging cacheable queries reduces overhead. Similarly, log file rotation and backpressure handling in Logstash pipelines safeguard against data loss and service disruptions.

Security and Access Control

Redis credentials should be handled cautiously, especially when interacting with exporters. Enabling TLS and role-based access controls on Redis instances prevents unauthorized access to telemetry data or operational commands that could affect service availability.

Future Directions

Emerging standards in OpenTelemetry provide enhanced frameworks for instrumenting Redis and related components with distributed tracing. Combining metrics, logs, and traces within a unified observability model promises finer-grained insights and automated root cause analysis capabilities.

By systematically incorporating Redis into centralized observability and monitoring pipelines, organizations gain comprehensive visibility over cache and data access layers that are critical to modern cloud-native application performance and reliability. Proper configuration, monitoring, and visualization enable proactive maintenance, rapid incident detection, and informed capacity planning.

8.4. Orchestrating Redis with Containers and Kubernetes

Deploying Redis in containerized environments, particularly with Docker and Kubernetes, introduces a transformative approach to scalability, resilience, and operational management. This section delineates pragmatic patterns for containerizing Redis, implementing automated failover strategies, ensuring persistent data management, and leveraging Helm charts for streamlined deployments within Kubernetes clusters.

Containerizing Redis: Docker Patterns

Redis containerization begins with crafting an optimized Docker image, either leveraging the official `redis` image or extending it to incorporate custom configurations and monitoring tools. Essential patterns include:

- **Minimal base image:** Starting from the official `redis:alpine` image reduces attack surface and resource usage.

- **Immutable configuration:** Embed Redis configuration files in the image or mount them as ConfigMaps in Kubernetes, ensuring declarative control over behavior.

- **Health checks:** Implement both `HEALTHCHECK` directives in Dockerfiles and readiness/liveness probes in Kubernetes to detect malfunctioning instances promptly.

- **Resource constraints:** Define CPU and memory limits

to prevent resource contention, particularly critical in multi-tenant or resource-constrained environments.

The combination of these practices results in stateless, immutable Redis containers that can be deployed repeatedly with predictable configurations and testable behaviors.

Scalability via Kubernetes StatefulSets

Redis deployments require a nuanced orchestration pattern to manage scaling and state persistence. Kubernetes StatefulSets offer a controlled mechanism to manage multiple Redis nodes while maintaining stable network identities and storage bindings. Key considerations include:

- **Stable network identities:** Each Redis pod receives a persistent hostname, essential for cluster nodes to communicate reliably in sharded or replicated topologies.

- **Persistent storage volumes:** Use PersistentVolume-Claims (PVCs) to attach storage to each pod, ensuring data durability even when pods are rescheduled or restarted.

- **Pod ordering and lifecycle hooks:** StatefulSets guarantee an ordered startup and termination sequence, crucial for Redis cluster initialization and graceful shutdowns.

An exemplar StatefulSet manifest snippet defining volume mounts and readiness probes might include:

```
apiVersion: apps/v1
kind: StatefulSet
metadata:
  name: redis
spec:
  serviceName: "redis"
  replicas: 3
  selector:
    matchLabels:
      app: redis
  template:
```

```
metadata:
  labels:
    app: redis
spec:
  containers:
  - name: redis
    image: redis:6.2-alpine
    ports:
    - containerPort: 6379
    volumeMounts:
    - name: data
      mountPath: /data
    readinessProbe:
      exec:
        command:
        - redis-cli
        - ping
      initialDelaySeconds: 5
      periodSeconds: 10
volumeClaimTemplates:
- metadata:
    name: data
  spec:
    accessModes: [ "ReadWriteOnce" ]
    resources:
      requests:
        storage: 5Gi
```

Automated Failover and High Availability

High availability for Redis, especially when deployed in Kubernetes, mandates the integration of automated failover mechanisms
to mitigate node failures and ensure continuous service availability.
Two primary approaches arise:

- **Redis Sentinel:** A lightweight, distributed system that continuously monitors Redis nodes, detects failures, and orchestrates leader elections for failover. Sentinel is compatible
  with StatefulSets and can be deployed as sidecar containers
  or separate pods. Incorporate Sentinel readiness checks and
  configure quorum settings carefully to balance responsiveness and false-positive avoidance.

- **Redis Cluster mode:** Redis Cluster natively partitions
  data across multiple nodes with automatic failover capabil-

ities. Kubernetes operators supporting Redis Cluster can automate node addition/removal and rebalancing, simplifying operational overhead.

Best practices for failover configuration in Kubernetes include utilizing separate dedicated pods for Sentinel processes, applying PodDisruptionBudgets to maintain quorum, and leveraging operator tooling for automated health monitoring and healing.

Persistent Data Management

Ensuring Redis data persistence in orchestration environments requires judicious use of Kubernetes storage abstractions. Key patterns include:

- **Stateful data volumes:** As shown in StatefulSet examples, PersistentVolumeClaims bind storage to Redis pods, providing durability across pod restarts.

- **Storage class selection:** Selecting performant and highly available storage backends-such as SSD-backed network storage with replication-underpins Redis durability and performance.

- **Backup and restore workflows:** Regular snapshots facilitated by Redis `BGSAVE` commands or RDB/AOF backups need to be orchestrated externally, frequently leveraging Kubernetes CronJobs to automate backup schedules and storage cleanup.

- **Data encryption:** Encrypting data at rest, either natively supported by the storage provider or via filesystem-level encryption, protects sensitive in-memory datasets when persisted.

Combining persistent storage with robust backup pipelines prevents catastrophic data loss and enables stateful recovery in production-grade systems.

Helm: Efficient Redis Deployment and Lifecycle Management

Helm serves as the de facto package manager for Kubernetes, simplifying complex Redis deployments while supporting reusable, configurable templates. Optimal approaches include:

- **Using stable Helm charts:** Leverage trusted community charts, such as those maintained by Bitnami or the official Redis Helm chart, which encapsulate best practices for resource sizing, pod management, and service exposure.

- **Custom values overrides:** Customize replicas, persistence parameters, resource limits, and security contexts through the `values.yaml` file, enabling environment-specific deployments without modifying base charts.

- **Lifecycle hooks and upgrade strategies:** Helm charts can define pre-install, post-install, pre-upgrade, and post-upgrade hooks, facilitating seamless schema migrations, configuration reloads, or data transformation during version upgrades.

- **Version pinning and rollback:** Track chart versions explicitly to ensure repeatability and enable rollback capabilities, crucial in environments demanding high reliability.

A typical Helm command for deploying Redis with persistence enabled might resemble:

```
helm install redis bitnami/redis --set persistence.enabled=true \
  --set replica.replicaCount=3 --namespace redis
```

This invocation provisions a three-replica Redis cluster with persistent storage, based on the Bitnami chart, providing a solid foundation for production workloads.

Operational Lifecycle and Monitoring

193

Maintaining Redis deployments in Kubernetes requires vigilant operational practices:

- **Monitoring and alerting:** Integrate Prometheus exporters for Redis metrics, including memory usage, command statistics, and latency. Pair with alertmanager rules for proactive incident detection.

- **Logging:** Redirect Redis logs to standard output to enable centralized collection through Kubernetes-native tools like Fluentd or Elasticsearch.

- **Rolling updates and zero-downtime deployments:** Employ Kubernetes deployment strategies that maintain availability by sequentially updating pods with readiness gating.

- **Security best practices:** Enforce RBAC policies limiting access to Redis pods and secrets, enable TLS encryption for client-server communication, and segregate networks using Kubernetes NetworkPolicies.

Regular health audits, combined with automated failover and backup routines, form the backbone of resilient Redis orchestration in containerized environments.

8.5. Data Migration and ETL Pipelines

Data migration in Redis-centric architectures involves transferring datasets between Redis instances or from disparate external data stores into Redis, often under stringent requirements for consistency, minimal downtime, and incremental updates. Such migrations are critical during system upgrades, scaling operations, cloud migrations, or integration of heterogeneous data sources. A thorough understanding of Redis's native features and third-party tooling is necessary to orchestrate these workflows effectively.

When migrating data between Redis instances, the primary challenges include preserving atomicity of data sets, avoiding service interruption, and efficiently handling live updates. Redis provides several mechanisms to facilitate this. The MIGRATE command enables direct key-wise transfer from a source to a destination Redis server, working atomically on individual keys while supporting blocking or non-blocking behaviors depending on context. However, bulk migration via MIGRATE can be impractical for large data volumes or complex datasets because it operates key-wise singularly.

For larger datasets or zero-downtime migrations, the preferred workflow leverages Redis's *RDB* (Redis Database) snapshotting or the Append-Only File (AOF) persistence mechanism. Exporting an RDB snapshot from the source and importing it into the target allows a bulk, point-in-time data copy while the source remains operational. The disadvantage is the inherent static snapshot nature, which may cause data drift if the source is updated during migration. To alleviate this, incremental synchronization strategies are employed.

Incremental data migration can be orchestrated using Redis replication. By temporarily setting the target Redis instance as a replica of the source, the entire dataset and subsequent incremental changes are synchronized automatically. Once caught up, the replica can be promoted to a primary, minimizing downtime. This approach leverages Redis's built-in replication protocols to ensure consistency and durability without manual intervention.

When migrating data from external systems (SQL databases, NoSQL stores, filesystems) into Redis, Extract, Transform, Load (ETL) pipelines emerge as essential constructs. Redis's data model flexibility and rich datatype support (strings, hashes, lists, sets, sorted sets, streams) empower sophisticated transformations within these pipelines. ETL workflows typically extract raw data in batch or streaming modes, transform it to conform with Redis's schema and operational requirements, and finally load it into Redis in an optimized manner.

Redis Streams, introduced in recent versions, facilitate real-time ETL scenarios by acting as a persistent, log-like data structure for event-driven pipelines. Application components can produce and consume streams data, allowing transformations and enrichment to occur inline before loading into transactional or analytic Redis structures. This enables efficient near-real-time data ingestion and processing across distributed systems.

Transformation layers within ETL may involve key namespace restructuring, data type conversion, aggregation, or enrichment by joining with existing Redis data. For example, a user profile extracted from a relational database can be normalized and loaded as Redis hashes with secondary indices maintained as sorted sets or sets, enabling low-latency queries and real-time analytics.

Load optimization strategies are critical at scale. Redis's support for bulk commands such as MSET, HMSET, or pipeline batching considerably accelerates high-throughput data loading. Pipelining batches multiple commands to reduce network round-trips, ensuring efficient insertion rates while preventing client or server overload. Additionally, Redis Cluster's sharding capabilities allow parallel loading across multiple nodes, distributing both data and ETL processing workload.

Maintaining data consistency during ETL is ensured by atomicity at a command-level, combined with versioned or transactional synchronization patterns applied at the application level. When consistency guarantees must extend beyond a single Redis instance, tools such as RedisGears or Lua scripting enable orchestrating complex logic within Redis, controlling data mutations, validations, and conditional insertions atomically.

Downtime minimization during migration and ETL processes also involves careful resource management and monitoring. Progressive loading during low-traffic windows, gradual keyspace migration, and throttling ETL job execution help avoid overwhelming Redis instances. Monitoring Redis performance metrics such as memory usage, command latency, and replication lag provides feedback for adaptive tuning.

Data migration workflows leveraging Redis depend on a combination of native replication, snapshotting, and command-level operations designed to balance consistency and uptime. ETL pipelines are robustly supported by Redis's extensible datatype system and scripting capabilities, enabling efficient extraction from external sources, in-flight transformation, and optimized loading. This foundation allows Redis to function as a dynamic data store within complex, data-centric architectures requiring high availability and operational agility.

8.6. Redis in the Serverless Ecosystem

Serverless computing platforms epitomize the decoupling of application logic from underlying infrastructure management, enabling developers to deploy discrete, stateless functions that scale automatically in response to demand. This architectural paradigm presents inherent challenges for managing state, coordinating events, and ensuring low-latency data access within ephemeral compute environments. Redis, as an in-memory data structure store, addresses these challenges by serving as a high-performance, persistent layer that complements the transient nature of serverless functions.

Stateless Function State Management

Serverless functions, by design, are stateless and ephemeral, making it necessary to externalize any state that must persist across invocations. Redis provides an ideal external state store, delivering sub-millisecond latency and flexible data structures that align with common serverless state management patterns.

A typical pattern involves using Redis hashes, strings, or sorted sets to store and retrieve user session data, transactional context, or intermediate computation results. Functions interact with Redis synchronously on invocation to restore necessary state, perform computation, and then update the stored state asynchronously if required.

To illustrate, consider an AWS Lambda function responsible for processing a user shopping cart. Upon invocation, the function retrieves the cart's contents from Redis using a unique session identifier, processes item quantities or pricing, and writes back updated cart information. The separation of compute and state enables horizontal scaling of the Lambda function while Redis efficiently maintains consistent state across instances.

```python
import redis
import json

redis_client = redis.Redis(host='redis-server', port=6379)

def lambda_handler(event, context):
    session_id = event['session_id']
    cart_data = redis_client.get(session_id)
    cart = json.loads(cart_data) if cart_data else {}

    # Modify cart items
    cart['item_count'] = cart.get('item_count', 0) + event['
    add_item']

    # Persist updated cart
    redis_client.set(session_id, json.dumps(cart))

    return {"status": "success", "cart": cart}
```

Event-Driven Triggers and Messaging

Serverless architectures inherently benefit from event-driven communication patterns. Redis supports this model through its Publish/Subscribe (Pub/Sub) capabilities and the Redis Streams data type, both adaptable as efficient event buses within distributed serverless applications.

The Pub/Sub mechanism allows serverless functions to subscribe to channels representing application events, such as user actions or system status updates. When one function publishes a message on a channel, all subscribed functions receive the event in real time, enabling loosely coupled service interactions without persistent connections.

Redis Streams enhance these capabilities by persisting event data, offering reliable message delivery semantics crucial for serverless workflows where functions may be invoked sporadically or fail transiently. Streams support consumer groups, allowing multiple serverless function instances to coordinate processing of event data while maintaining message ordering and avoiding duplicate processing.

A practical example involves a serverless image processing pipeline. An upload event triggers a Lambda function to publish image metadata to a Redis stream. Downstream functions in consumer groups ingest stream entries, process the images, and publish processed results to other streams or update Redis keys, enabling scalable, asynchronous processing without centralized orchestration.

Automatic Scaling and Connection Management

Serverless platforms automatically scale compute resources in response to workload, which can result in an unbounded number of simultaneous function executions attempting to connect to external services. Managing Redis connections in these highly concurrent scenarios requires careful design to avoid overwhelming the Redis server or generating excessive connection overhead.

Connection pooling and lightweight clients help mitigate the impact of rapid scaling. In environments such as AWS Lambda, where function instances spin up and tear down rapidly, establishing persistent Redis connections is often infeasible. Instead, serverless functions typically open connections on-demand per invocation and leverage client libraries optimized for ephemeral usage patterns.

Furthermore, deploying Redis in a clustered mode or using managed Redis services with horizontal scaling capabilities can accommodate the bursty traffic characteristics of serverless workloads. Autoscaling Redis clusters dynamically balance load and maintain low latency, ensuring reliability under unpredictable function invocation patterns.

Bridging Ephemeral Compute and Persistent Fast Data

Redis acts as an essential bridging component in serverless applications by harmonizing ephemeral compute with persistent, fast-access data. Serverless functions focus on scalable, parallelized computation void of local state, offloading the requirement for data durability and inter-function coordination to Redis.

The flexible data structures inherent in Redis provide semantic richness to store counters, bitmaps, hyperloglogs, and streams-enabling sophisticated stateful computations and analytical capabilities to execute within a serverless context. Redis modules further expand use cases by enabling search, graph processing, and probabilistic data structures, which can scale seamlessly as backend services to function layers.

Overall, integrating Redis into serverless architectures empowers developers to construct systems that maintain high throughput and low latency while retaining the operational simplicity and cost-efficiency advantages intrinsic to serverless computing. Redis's in-memory persistence of application state and real-time eventing complement the elasticity of ephemeral functions, allowing complex workflows and stateful applications to thrive without compromising scalability or responsiveness.

Chapter 9

Emerging Patterns and Future Directions

The Redis story continues to evolve, transcending its origins as a simple cache to become the core of innovative digital platforms. In this chapter, peer into the frontier of what's possible with Redis—spotlighting breakthrough use cases, bold architectural patterns, and the roadmap that will shape tomorrow's data-driven world. Whether you're intrigued by AI, edge computing, or open source innovation, prepare to glimpse the future through the lens of Redis.

9.1. Redis Beyond Cache: Primary Database Patterns

Redis, traditionally perceived as an in-memory data structure store optimized for caching and transient data, has undergone significant evolution to assume roles more commonly reserved for primary databases. Advances in persistence capabilities, schema management, and durability now enable Redis to serve as the system of record in a variety of demanding application domains. This section examines the critical shifts in Redis's architecture and ecosystem that support this expanded role, as well as the fundamental challenges and design patterns emerging in primary database deployments.

A key enabler of Redis's transition from cache to primary database is its progressive persistence mechanisms, designed to balance in-memory speed with data durability. Redis offers two primary persistence options: snapshotting (RDB) and an append-only file (AOF). RDB performs point-in-time snapshots of in-memory data at configured intervals, providing a low-overhead recovery mechanism but with a potential for data loss during failure windows. Conversely, AOF logs each write command serialized to disk, enabling more granular recovery with lower data loss risk. Recent improvements enhance AOF's rewrite and fsync policies, minimizing latency spikes and ensuring consistent, write-ahead logging semantics. Moreover, hybrid persistence modes combine RDB snapshots with AOF logs, optimizing durability and recovery speed for production workloads demanding high availability.

Beyond persistence, Redis's native data model advances enable flexible schema management suited for complex applications. Unlike traditional relational databases, Redis's schema-free, key-value architecture supports multiple rich data types: strings, hashes, lists, sets, sorted sets, streams, and modules that can be composed to model intricate data relationships. Modules such as RedisJSON, RedisSearch, and RedisGraph extend this natively, enabling secondary indexing, full-text search, document storage, and graph queries while maintaining Redis's performance characteristics. This composability allows schema evolution without downtime or costly migrations, addressing the schema rigidity often associated with relational designs.

Durability in Redis as a primary data store is further enhanced through replication and high-availability solutions. Redis supports asynchronous primary-replica replication with configurable replica acknowledgement modes, allowing synchronous acknowledgment patterns that reduce the risk of acknowledged but non-persisted writes. Redis Sentinel and Redis Cluster facilitate automated failover and partitioning, ensuring resilience and horizontal scalability. However, adopting Redis as a system of record necessitates careful consideration of replication lag and split-brain scenarios. Strategies such as quorum-based write acknowledgement and employing Redis Cluster's slot-based partitioning provide mitigation paths, but inherent trade-offs between consistency, availability, and partition tolerance remain fundamental.

Core challenges arise when Redis is positioned as the primary database, particularly concerning transactional consistency and complex multi-key operations. Redis provides single-threaded atomicity for individual commands but lacks native support for multi-command ACID transactions typical in relational systems. The introduction of Lua scripting and the `MULTI/EXEC` command blocks partially address this, enabling atomic execution of custom command sequences. However, these constructs lack isolated, rollback-capable transactions with strict serializability guarantees. Application architects must therefore design data models and workflows that minimize cross-key dependencies or implement compensation logic for eventual consistency.

Another consideration is memory management and persistence cost. Maintaining an entire dataset in-memory to leverage Redis's performance can be costly and challenging at scale. Redis Enterprise and open-source variants support features like eviction policies, Redis on Flash, and tiered storage that retain hot working sets in memory while spilling cold data to persistent storage with minimal impact on query latency. These capabilities facilitate economically viable scaling of Redis as a primary database without sacrificing responsiveness.

Operational complexity often increases in primary database

deployments. Observability tools integrated into the Redis ecosystem-such as enhanced slow-log tracing, command statistics, and latency monitoring-augment traditional database metrics. Additionally, Redis modules and clients support transactional tracing and conflict detection, aiding debugging and consistency assurance. Yet, Redis's single-threaded core architecture demands careful capacity planning and workload profiling to avoid bottlenecks under high concurrency.

The maturity of Redis's persistence, schema flexibility, durability, and operational tooling has expanded its applicability as a primary database in distributed, latency-sensitive systems. While it does not supplant traditional relational or multi-model databases in scenarios requiring strict ACID compliance or complex joins, Redis's design patterns enable it to function effectively as a system of record where throughput, availability, and flexible data representations are paramount. Understanding and mitigating the inherent trade-offs within Redis's consistency, durability, and scaling models is essential for architectural success in these deployments.

9.2. AI/ML Feature Caching and Model Serving

Modern AI/ML systems demand rapid access to feature data and efficient model inference mechanisms to support real-time and large-scale applications. Redis, with its in-memory architecture and versatile data structures, has emerged as a foundational component in these pipelines, serving both as a high-speed feature store and an inference cache. This section elaborates on the integration of Redis in AI/ML workflows, emphasizing model versioning, online feature engineering, and real-time prediction capabilities.

Redis as a High-Speed Feature Store

In machine learning workflows, features often constitute the bulk of the data accessed during inference. Traditional storage systems, such as relational databases or disk-based key-value stores, impose latency penalties inconsistent with the needs of interactive or streaming inference. Redis addresses this limitation by holding feature vectors in memory, enabling sub-millisecond retrievals at scale.

Features are stored in Redis using various data structures optimized for different access patterns. Hashes allow grouping related features under one key corresponding to an entity ID, facilitating atomic read and update operations. Sorted sets can be exploited for time-series features where temporal ranking is essential. Additionally, Redis supports efficient bitmaps and HyperLogLogs for approximate counting features.

To maintain consistency between the feature store and offline data, Redis can be integrated into feature-flow pipelines where feature vectors are continuously updated based on streaming data. This enables online feature engineering where intermediate features are computed on-the-fly within Redis using Lua scripting or RedisGears, a serverless engine for running custom logic close to the data.

Model Versioning and Feature Evolution

Robust machine learning deployment requires systematic management of model versions alongside their respective feature sets. Redis facilitates this by namespacing keys with version tags that relate features and models tightly. For example, feature keys prefixed with the model version ID ensure that inference code accesses features compatible with the deployed model logic.

Furthermore, Redis' support for transactions and multi-key atomic operations allows feature updates and model swaps to occur synchronously, eliminating inconsistent states during rollouts. This capability is crucial when performing A/B testing or gradual traffic shifting between model versions, allowing for smooth transitions without downtime or serving stale data.

Redis modules also extend the core system with capabilities for metadata tagging and schema validation, enabling the enforcement of feature contracts tied to model versions. This ensures that the inference layer does not consume incompatible or deprecated features, reducing potential model degradation due to data drift.

Online Feature Engineering and Real-Time Inference

Online feature engineering refers to the computation and transformation of raw input data into feature representations in real time, directly preceding model inference. Redis supports this paradigm by leveraging its native Lua scripting to perform lightweight feature transformations atomically during feature retrieval. For instance, normalization, aggregation, and interaction terms can be computed in the same memory context as feature fetching, thereby eliminating costly roundtrips between systems.

RedisGears extends this capability by enabling complex workflows that respond to streams, database changes, or scheduled triggers. Such workflows can implement online feature joins, windowed aggregations, and enrichment from external data sources. The rapid execution environment offered by RedisGears ensures minimal latency impact during inference.

For serving model predictions, Redis acts as an inference cache where output results of frequently executed model queries are stored keyed by input feature hashes or query signatures. This cache avoids redundant model invocations for repeated queries, thus improving throughput and reducing execution costs. TTL (time to live) controls enforce the freshness of cached predictions, balancing latency and accuracy requirements.

Scaling Real-Time Predictions with Redis

To serve millions of predictions per second, Redis supports horizontal scaling through clustering and partitioning. Model state and feature data are sharded across nodes with consistent hashing to distribute workload evenly. This allows the caching layer and feature retrieval to scale linearly without introducing bottlenecks.

Redis' replication mechanisms provide high availability and disaster recovery, critical for production AI/ML systems requiring uninterrupted service. Combined with careful client-side request routing, this architecture ensures both low latency and fault tolerance.

Finally, Redis integrates with modern container orchestration and monitoring tools, enabling dynamic resource allocation based on inference load. Metrics exported by Redis, such as hit rates, latency percentiles, and throughput, inform autoscaling policies that maintain optimal cost-performance balance.

```python
import redis
import hashlib
import json

r = redis.Redis(host='redis-server', port=6379, db=0)

def get_features(entity_id, model_version):
    feature_key = f"model:{model_version}:features:{entity_id}"
    features = r.hgetall(feature_key)
    if not features:
        # Fallback logic to fetch from cold store or recompute
        return None
    return {k.decode(): float(v) for k, v in features.items()}

def generate_cache_key(features):
    feature_str = json.dumps(features, sort_keys=True)
    return hashlib.sha256(feature_str.encode()).hexdigest()

def get_prediction(entity_id, model_version, model_infer_func):
    features = get_features(entity_id, model_version)
    if features is None:
        return None
    cache_key = f"model:{model_version}:predictions:{
     generate_cache_key(features)}"
    prediction = r.get(cache_key)
    if prediction:
        return float(prediction)
    # Run model inference as fallback
    pred_value = model_infer_func(features)
    # Cache result with TTL for 5 minutes
    r.setex(cache_key, 300, pred_value)
```

```
    return pred_value
```

```
Sample output for entity_id=123 and model_version=v2.1:
Features fetched: {'age': 35.0, 'income': 75000.0, 'visit_count': 10.0}
Cache miss - running model inference
Prediction cached with key: model:v2.1:predictions:c1a456...
Prediction result: 0.87
```

By leveraging Redis as a unified, low-latency platform for feature storage, online transformations, and inference result caching, AI/ML systems can achieve scalable real-time prediction performance. Combined with disciplined versioning and operational management, this approach reduces complexity and accelerates iteration cycles in production machine learning environments.

9.3. Edge and IoT Architectures

In contemporary distributed systems, the integration of Redis at the network edge and within Internet of Things (IoT) deployments introduces novel architectural patterns that address critical challenges such as intermittent connectivity, local data aggregation, and decentralized decision-making. These paradigms leverage Redis's in-memory data structures and replication capabilities to enable robust, efficient, and secure operations across geographically dispersed devices, contributing to enhanced system responsiveness and resilience.

At the network edge, devices often operate in environments where consistent cloud connectivity cannot be guaranteed. Redis can be deployed locally on edge gateways or even on suitably provisioned end devices to act as an ephemeral data store that buffers sensor readings, command queues, and contextual metadata. This approach mitigates latency and bandwidth constraints by enabling local processing and caching before synchronization with central cloud repositories. The use of Redis's data structures, such as streams and sorted sets, facilitates time-ordered event storage and priority scheduling, respectively, enabling real-time analytics and control loops directly on-site.

A key pattern in these deployments is local data aggregation, where Redis instances collect and preprocess raw IoT data to reduce the volume transmitted upstream. For example, edge devices can implement aggregation logic using Redis Lua scripts or apply data reduction through approximate data structures like HyperLogLog or Bloom filters integrated natively within Redis modules. This not only minimizes network load but also accelerates downstream analytics by transmitting enriched and distilled information. Aggregation can further be customized to suit application semantics, such as hourly averaging of environmental sensor data or event anomaly detection.

Decentralized decision-making emerges as a natural extension facilitated by Redis's support for pub/sub messaging and lightweight transactions. Edge nodes can exchange state updates and alerts via Redis channels to coordinate collective responses without centralized orchestration. This model promotes fault tolerance, enabling devices to proceed autonomously during connectivity degradation or cloud outages. To implement such workflows, transactions based on Redis's optimistic locking mechanisms (WATCH/-MULTI/EXEC) ensure atomic updates to shared state, preserving consistency in concurrent environments.

Synchronization between distributed Redis instances in edge and cloud tiers introduces complexity due to network unreliability and device heterogeneity. Redis Replication and Redis Sentinel provide foundational constructs for high availability and failover but require augmentation for multi-master or mesh topologies typical in edge and IoT scenarios. Emerging synchronization strategies include conflict-free replicated data types (CRDTs) supported by third-party modules, which allow eventual consistency without centralized conflict resolution. Furthermore, asynchronous synchronization can be orchestrated via custom scripts or external orchestrators that reconcile divergent data states during periodic connectivity windows, preserving data integrity while tolerating temporary partitions.

Data locality remains central to performance optimization and cost reduction in edge-IoT systems. By retaining frequently accessed data and computation near the source, Redis instances reduce roundtrip times and cloud dependency. This approach is essential in applications with strict real-time constraints, such as industrial automation or autonomous vehicles, where milliseconds matter. Redis Enterprise products often extend this concept with active-active geo-distribution, enabling seamless data access across multiple edge and cloud sites while maintaining consistency guarantees tailored to use cases.

Security considerations in these distributed architectures are multifaceted. At the edge, devices are more exposed to physical and network attacks, necessitating robust authentication and encryption. Redis supports TLS and ACL (Access Control Lists) to restrict command access and secure communication channels. Additionally, deploying Redis instances within trusted execution environments or containerized microservices enhances isolation. Device identity management integrated with mutual TLS or hardware-based attestation strengthens trust in decentralized ecosystems.

Data privacy regulations impose further constraints on data residency and processing locality, which edge-based Redis architectures inherently facilitate by limiting sensitive data transmission to cloud environments. Encryption-at-rest and fine-grained role-based access controls contribute to compliance. From a network perspective, segmented local networks with firewall policies constrain attack surfaces, while periodic auditing and logging mechanisms can monitor unusual access patterns.

Redis enables flexible and powerful design patterns for edge and IoT architectures that confront intermittent connectivity, optimize local computations, and enforce decentralized coordination. Synchronization models extend Redis's core replication capabilities to mesh and eventually consistent topologies. Data locality is leveraged to improve responsiveness and reduce cloud dependency, while comprehensive security practices mitigate risks inherent in distributed deployments. These innovations collectively empower architects and engineers to construct scalable, resilient, and efficient edge-IoT systems that adapt dynamically to operational constraints and performance demands.

9.4. Multi-Region and Multi-Cloud Redis

Deploying Redis across multiple geographic regions and cloud platforms presents a complex intersection of distributed systems challenges, including consistency, latency optimization, failover robustness, and regulatory compliance. Such deployments serve the demands of globally distributed applications requiring low-latency access, high availability, and resilience to regional failures, while conforming to diverse data sovereignty regulations. The following analysis elucidates key design considerations and strategies to address these challenges effectively.

Data Consistency Models in Multi-Region Deployments

Redis's inherent single-node design guarantees strong consistency locally, but scaling this guarantee across global deployments necessitates carefully selected data replication and synchronization models. The central tension lies between strong consistency and availability governed by the CAP theorem, exacerbated over high-latency and potentially partition-prone WAN links.

One common approach is asynchronous replication, where a primary Redis instance located in one region replicates to read-only replicas in other regions. This architecture optimizes for low-latency reads across regions but introduces eventual consistency. Applications relying on this model must tolerate stale reads or implement conflict resolution at the application level.

Conversely, to achieve stronger consistency, distributed consensus protocols can be integrated atop Redis clusters, though at the cost of increased write latency. Emerging tools such as CRDT (Conflict-free Replicated Data Types) frameworks allow eventual consistency with mathematically bounded conflict resolution, which can be layered on Redis structures to facilitate concurrent multi-master updates with eventual convergence.

Hybrid models are also viable, where write operations requiring strict consistency are directed to a primary region, whereas read-heavy workloads leverage regional replicas. Redis Enterprise and other advanced Redis distributions support active-active geo-replication, which enables multi-master writes with conflict detection and resolution handled at the database layer.

Latency Minimization and Topology Design

Minimizing latency in multi-region Redis architectures hinges on the strategic placement of nodes and the routing of requests. Since Redis is predominantly a memory-resident data store optimized for low-latency access, network latency dominates in inter-region communication.

A common topology involves a regionally local Redis cluster serving low-latency reads and writes, backed by asynchronous replication from a designated primary region. Edge caching layers or CDN integrations can further localize frequently accessed data. For write-heavy global workloads, the deployment of multi-master Redis setups with application logic or middleware to partition data by geographic ownership can reduce cross-region write latency.

Latency-aware client libraries and intelligent DNS routing are crucial to ensure traffic is directed to the nearest regional Redis endpoint. Additionally, employing network acceleration techniques such as private inter-region links, optimized TCP stacks, and connection pooling reduces communication overhead over the WAN.

For multi-cloud environments, latency considerations extend to inter-cloud network performance, which is often variable and less predictable than intra-cloud links. Multi-cloud Redis deployments must be architected with awareness of network SLA variations and incorporate mechanisms for dynamic failover and traffic rerouting.

High Availability and Failover Mechanisms

Ensuring availability in distributed Redis requires architecting for both regional outages and cloud provider failures. Multi-region replication inherently provides geographic redundancy, but failover complexity increases with the number of regions and cloud platforms involved.

Redis Sentinel and Redis Cluster provide native failover capabilities within a single cloud or region, but these solutions lack native cross-region failover. Cross-region failover typically necessitates orchestrated external tooling or Redis Enterprise features supporting active-active and active-passive failover modes with health monitoring.

Failover strategies must address split-brain scenarios, where partitions lead to concurrent primaries in different regions. Techniques such as quorum-based leader election with consensus protocols help mitigate such issues. Additionally, automated detection of region-level failures coupled with rerouting clients to healthy clusters ensures business continuity.

Data loss risk during failover can be minimized by selecting replication methods that guarantee durability, such as synchronous replication with fallback reads. However, synchronous replication across regions negatively impacts write latency; hence, asynchronous replication with automated repair processes post-failover is often the pragmatic compromise.

Compliance and Data Sovereignty Considerations

Multi-region and multi-cloud Redis deployments must navigate the complexities of global data governance frameworks such as GDPR, CCPA, and other national data residency laws. These regulations often mandate that specific data categories remain within defined geographic boundaries or require strict auditing and logging of access and modification.

Architecting Redis solutions to meet these requirements typically involves selective data locality controls, partitioning data by jurisdiction, and employing encryption at rest and in transit. Certain Redis modules and enterprise offerings provide role-based access control (RBAC) and detailed audit trails to support compliance.

A multi-cloud approach introduces additional challenges as data traverses different providers' networks and infrastructure. Organizations commonly deploy discrete Redis clusters per cloud region, employing secure VPN or dedicated interconnects that ensure encrypted and auditable data flows. Compliance automation tools can enforce policies that prevent unauthorized cross-region data replication.

Summary of Strategic Trade-Offs

Multi-region, multi-cloud Redis architectures must balance trade-offs among consistency, latency, availability, and compliance. The choice between eventual and strong consistency governs replication schemes, while geographic topology and network design influence latency and failover complexity. Compliance mandates impose constraints on data placement and access logging, shaping infrastructure segmentation and security mechanisms.

Emerging Redis-based distributed databases and advanced geo-replication capabilities offer promising solutions but require a nuanced understanding of the interplay of distributed systems theory, network architecture, and regulatory landscape. Effective global Redis deployments integrate these considerations into a coherent strategy aligned with application requirements and operational capabilities.

9.5. Contributions from the Open Source Community

The open source community has played an instrumental role in evolving Redis beyond its initial scope as an in-memory key-value store. This dynamic ecosystem, fueled by contributors from around the world, continuously extends Redis's core capabilities through innovative modules, specialized data types, operational tooling, and diverse third-party integrations that collectively enhance Redis's utility and adaptability across numerous application domains.

One of the most striking aspects of community contributions is the development of custom data types designed to enrich Redis's native structures such as strings, lists, sets, hashes, and sorted sets. Modules like RedisBloom introduce probabilistic data structures such as Bloom filters, Cuckoo filters, Count-Min Sketches, and Top-K lists, enabling memory-efficient approximate set membership and frequency counts essential for large-scale analytics and caching systems. Similarly, RedisGraph incorporates graph database functionality by implementing the GraphBLAS specification, allowing complex graph queries and traversals directly within Redis. This expands Redis's applicability to social networks, recommendation engines, and fraud detection-domains previously requiring separate graph-oriented technologies.

Community-driven modules such as RedisJSON bring rich JSON document handling capabilities to Redis. By enabling in-place manipulation and querying of JSON data without serialization overhead, these extensions support modern web and mobile applications that depend on flexible, schema-less document stores. This tight integration of JSON within Redis leverages native server-side data manipulation commands, resulting in both performance gains and simplified application architectures.

Enhancements that facilitate operational excellence form another significant pillar of community innovation. Tools like RedisInsight, although officially supported, grew from early community efforts to provide an advanced graphical interface for monitoring, querying, and optimizing Redis instances. Complementary to core management tools, community projects such as Redis-trib and redis-cli extensions have historically enabled ease of cluster administration, failover handling, and latency profiling. These operational toolkits empower administrators to maintain high availability and performance in complex Redis deployments, capabilities critical as Redis usage scales in enterprise environments.

Third-party integrations reflect Redis's ecosystem diversity, connecting it to broader platforms and languages. Libraries and connectors crafted by the community bridge Redis with machine learning frameworks, message brokers, and serverless architectures. For instance, Python's redis-py and Node.js's ioredis offer asynchronous, multi-threaded, and cluster-aware clients enabling seamless integration into modern microservices landscapes. On the backend, exporters for monitoring systems such as Prometheus, developed and maintained by community contributors, facilitate robust observability of Redis metrics within heterogeneous infrastructure.

The open source landscape for Redis modules is also distinguished by its freedom to innovate on operational semantics and performance characteristics. Some community projects explore novel persistence models or introduce advanced eviction policies tailored for specific workloads. For example, customized modules implement time series data management, enabling aggregations and downsampling natively within Redis, reducing reliance on external processing tools. These innovations demonstrate the community's ongoing effort to tailor Redis to niche use cases while maintaining interoperability with standard deployments.

Collaboration within the community frequently materializes through an open governance model, shared code repositories, and conference events like RedisConf. This culture encourages contribution, quality feedback, and peer review, which elevates code robustness and feature completeness. The modular architecture of Redis itself facilitates this model, as contributors can experiment and deploy functionality independently of the official Redis server release cycle, accelerating innovation velocity.

Moreover, the synergy between the core Redis development team and the open source community ensures that successful community modules often influence the core roadmap or become candidates for official support. This dynamic fosters a virtuous cycle wherein ideas incubated in the community mature through real-world usage and iterative refinement, then contribute back to the upstream product. Examples include the eventual incorporation of cluster support and stream data types, which were heavily shaped by community experimentation before full official adoption.

In summary, the Redis open source community introduces not only new features but also operational sophistication and ecosystem integrations that collectively broaden Redis's horizon. By continuously expanding the capabilities of data types, improving tooling, and fostering interoperability, these independent yet coordinated contributions have transformed Redis into a versatile platform suitable for a broad spectrum of use cases ranging from caching and session management to real-time analytics and graph processing. The community's vibrancy and technical excellence remain key drivers in sustaining Redis's prominence and its evolution as a foundational technology in distributed computing.

9.6. The Roadmap: Redis in the Next Decade

Redis's evolution continues to be shaped by the convergence of performance demands, versatility, and the expanding complexity of modern applications. As indicated by its maintainers and key contributors, the roadmap for Redis over the next decade targets significant advancements not only in the core engine but also in the ecosystem's breadth and operational best practices. These anticipated developments orient Redis toward strengthened architectural scalability, enriched data model capabilities, and deeper integration with distributed computing paradigms.

At the core level, one of the foremost trajectories involves enhanced modularization and extensibility. Redis's module framework, introduced in recent years, has proven transformative by enabling the community to extend functionality without altering core code. Future efforts will prioritize making the core more lightweight and decoupled, facilitating faster innovation cycles through modules while preserving Redis's hallmark high performance and low latency. This will likely include a more formalized ABI (Application Binary Interface) for modules, enabling binary compatibility and easing long-term maintenance. Module isolation, potentially via sandboxing, is another anticipated feature, designed to improve stability and security when running third-party extensions.

In parallel, memory efficiency remains a prime concern. As datasets grow exponentially, improvements in internal data encoding and compression will become increasingly vital. Redis is expected to adopt more adaptive hybrid data structures that optimize for both memory and speed dynamically, depending on access patterns. Techniques such as compact encoding of sorted sets and better delta compression for streams and lists may become standard features. These innovations will extend Redis's suitability for embedded and edge environments where resource constraints dictate stringent memory budgets.

Sharding and scaling capabilities are also central to Redis's architectural evolution. With Redis Cluster as the current de facto horizontal scaling solution, future developments aim to provide more automated and intelligent cluster management. This includes self-healing nodes, dynamic slot rebalancing with minimal impact on availability, and advanced failure detection algorithms utilizing machine learning to prevent false positives and enable timely recovery. Integration with cloud-native orchestration systems and support for multi-tenancy at scale will further enhance Redis's role in complex enterprise deployments and global distributed systems.

On the data model front, the upcoming decade promises more sophisticated native support for graph data, time-series operations, and probabilistic data structures within Redis modules. Enhanced stream processing frameworks embedded in Redis will facilitate real-time event handling and complex analytics without external dependencies. These additions are expected to blur the lines between caching, database functionalities, and real-time data pipelines, positioning Redis as a versatile platform for converged data processing workloads.

The Redis ecosystem is also projected to expand profoundly. Official client libraries will evolve toward richer feature sets, including support for reactive paradigms and seamless telemetry integration. Tooling for observability will integrate deeply with distributed tracing systems, enabling granular visibility into command latencies and cluster-wide performance metrics. Development environments and debugging interfaces will become more sophisticated, assisting developers in profiling queries and tuning performance at scale. Moreover, Redis's growing compatibility with popular orchestration and service meshes will stimulate hybrid cloud and edge use cases.

Best practices for Redis deployment and operation are likely to mature alongside these technical advancements. The maintainers advocate for enhanced automation of routine tasks such as backup, failover, and configuration tuning based on workload characterization. The adoption of Infrastructure as Code (IaC) paradigms and declarative configuration in Redis management will be more widespread. Additionally, new standards in security, including automated encryption key rotation and role-based access controls at a granular command level, are anticipated. These improvements will be critical as Redis becomes a core component in highly regulated industries where governance and compliance are paramount.

Architecturally, a fundamental shift toward a polyglot persistence model may emerge, enabling Redis nodes to natively coordinate with other databases and storage systems. Through advanced transaction and consistency protocols, Redis will likely operate as both a high-speed cache and a source of truth. Such integration could exploit upcoming hardware trends, including persistent memory technologies and high-throughput networking, pushing Redis beyond its current in-memory constraints.

In essence, Redis's trajectory over the coming decade is driven by a profound commitment to scalability, modularity, and operational resilience. These enhancements will not only enrich the core engine's performance characteristics but also foster a vibrant ecosystem that aligns with emerging application architectures. As Redis embraces greater diversity in workloads—ranging from ephemeral caching to durable real-time data processing—it will reinforce its role as an indispensable component in the next generation of distributed systems.

www.ingramcontent.com/pod-product-compliance
Lightning Source LLC
Chambersburg PA
CBHW061247220326
41599CB00028B/5564